MW00636884

GENERAL CONFERENCE ADDRESSES

GENERAL CONFERENCE ADDRESSES

JOURNAL EDITION
OCTOBER 2020

DESERET BOOK
SALT LAKE CITY, UTAH

Book design © Deseret Book Company
Cover photo: Piotr Krzeslak/Shutterstock.com.
Interior photos: page 1, S.Borisov/Shutterstock.com; page 41, Romolo Tavani/Shutterstock.com; page 82, Smileus/Shutterstock.com; page 112, Yevhenii Chulovskyi/Shutterstock.com; page 147, Subbotina Anna/Shutterstock.com.

October 2020 General Conference Addresses, Journal Edition by Deseret Book Company © by Intellectual Reserve, Inc.

All rights reserved. No part of this book may be reproduced in any form or by any means without permission in writing from the publisher, Deseret Book Company, at permissions@deseretbook.com or PO Box 30178, Salt Lake City, Utah 84130.

This product, offered by Deseret Book Company, is neither made nor endorsed by Intellectual Reserve, Inc., or The Church of Jesus Christ of Latter-day Saints.

Deseret Book is a registered trademark of Deseret Book Company.

Visit us at deseretbook.com

ISBN 978-1-62972-887-2

Printed in the United States of America
Artistic Printing, Salt Lake City, UT

10 9 8 7 6 5 4 3 2 1

CONTENTS

SATURDAY MORNING SESSION

SATURDAY AFTERNOON SESSION

WOMEN'S SESSION

SUNDAY MORNING SESSION

SUNDAY AFTERNOON SESSION

SATURDAY MORNING SESSION

OCTOBER 3, 2020

MOVING FORWARD

PRESIDENT RUSSELL M. NELSON

President of The Church of Jesus Christ of Latter-day Saints

My dear brothers and sisters, what a *joy* it is to be with you as we begin the 190th Semiannual General Conference of The Church of Jesus Christ of Latter-day Saints. I love joining with you in your homes or wherever you are to listen together to the messages of prophets, seers, and revelators and other Church leaders.

How grateful we are for the technology that allows us to be connected as one great worldwide gathering of disciples of Jesus Christ. General conference last April was viewed by more people than any preceding it, and we have every expectation that will happen again.

During the past few months, a global pandemic, raging wildfires, and other natural disasters have turned our world upside down. I grieve with each of you who has lost a loved one during this time. And I pray for all who are currently suffering.

Meanwhile, the work of the Lord is steadily moving forward. Amid social distancing, face masks, and Zoom meetings, we have learned to do some things differently and some even more effectively. Unusual times can bring unusual rewards.

Our missionaries and mission leaders have been resourceful, resilient, and truly remarkable. Although most missionaries have had to find new, creative ways to do their work, many missions have reported doing *more* teaching than ever.

We had to close temples for a time, and some construction projects were briefly delayed, but now they are all moving forward. In the calendar year 2020, we will have broken ground for 20 new temples!

Family history work has increased exponentially. Many new wards and stakes have been created. And we are gratified to report that the Church has provided pandemic humanitarian aid for 895 projects in 150 countries.

Increased gospel study in many homes is resulting in stronger testimonies and family relationships. One mother wrote: "We feel much closer to our children and grandchildren now that we gather on Zoom every Sunday. Each takes a turn giving their thoughts on *Come, Follow Me.* Prayers for our family members have changed because we better understand what they need."

I pray that we as a people are using this unique time to grow spiritually. We are here on earth to be tested, to see if we will choose to follow Jesus Christ, to repent regularly, to learn, and to progress. Our spirits long to progress. And we do that best by staying firmly on the covenant path.

Through it all, our Heavenly Father and His Son, Jesus Christ, love us! They care for us! They and Their holy angels are watching over us.[1] I know that is true.

As we gather to hear the words the Lord has inspired His servants to deliver, I invite you to ponder a promise the Lord made. He declared that "*whosoever will* may lay hold upon the word of God, which is quick and powerful, which shall divide asunder all the cunning . . . and the wiles of the devil, and lead the [disciple] of Christ in a strait and narrow course."[2]

I pray that you will *choose* to lay hold upon the word of God as it is declared during this general conference. And I pray that you may feel the Lord's perfect love for you,[3] in the sacred name of Jesus Christ, amen.

Notes

1. See Doctrine and Covenants 84:88.
2. Helaman 3:29; emphasis added.
3. See 2 Nephi 1:15.

WE WILL PROVE THEM HEREWITH (ABRAHAM 3:25)

ELDER DAVID A. BEDNAR
Of the Quorum of the Twelve Apostles

I pray for the assistance of the Holy Ghost for all of us as I share the thoughts and feelings that have come to my mind and heart in preparation for this general conference.

The Importance of Tests

For more than two decades before my call to full-time Church service, I worked as a university teacher and administrator. My primary responsibility as a teacher was to help students learn how to learn for themselves. And a vital element of my work was creating, grading, and providing feedback about student performance on tests. As you may already know from personal experience, tests typically are not the part of the learning process that students like the most!

But periodic tests absolutely are essential to learning. An effective test helps us to compare what we need to know with what we actually know about a specific subject; it also provides a standard against which we can evaluate our learning and development.

Likewise, tests in the school of mortality are a vital element of our eternal progression. Interestingly, however, the word *test* is not found even one time in the scriptural text of the standard works in English. Rather, words such as *prove, examine,* and *try* are used to describe various patterns of demonstrating appropriately our spiritual knowledge about, understanding of, and devotion to our Heavenly Father's eternal plan of happiness and our capacity to seek for the blessings of the Savior's Atonement.

He who authored the plan of salvation described the very purpose of our mortal probation using the words *prove, examine,* and *try* in ancient and modern scripture. "And we will *prove* them herewith, to see if they will do all things whatsoever the Lord their God shall command them."[1]

Consider this pleading by the Psalmist David:

"*Examine* me, O Lord, and *prove* me; *try* my reins and my heart.

"For thy lovingkindness is before mine eyes: and I have walked in thy truth."[2]

And the Lord declared in 1833, "Therefore, be not afraid of your enemies, for I have decreed in my heart, saith the Lord, that I will *prove* you in all things, whether you will abide in my covenant, even unto death, that you may be found worthy."[3]

Present-Day Proving and Trying

The year 2020 has been marked, in part, by a global pandemic that has proved, examined, and tried us in many ways. I pray that we as individuals and families are learning the valuable lessons that only challenging experiences can teach us. I also hope that all of us will more fully acknowledge the "greatness of God" and the truth that "he shall consecrate [our] afflictions for [our] gain."[4]

Two basic principles can guide and strengthen us as we face proving and trying circumstances in our lives, whatever they may be: (1) the principle of preparation and (2) the principle of pressing forward with a steadfastness in Christ.

Proving and Preparation

As disciples of the Savior, we are commanded to "*prepare every needful thing;* and establish a house, even a house of prayer, a house of fasting, a house of faith, a house of learning, a house of glory, a house of order, a house of God."[5]

We also are promised that "if ye are prepared ye shall not fear.

"And that ye might escape the power of the enemy, and be gathered unto me a righteous people, without spot and blameless."[6]

These scriptures provide a perfect framework for organizing and preparing our lives and homes both temporally and spiritually. Our efforts to prepare for the proving experiences of mortality should follow the example of the Savior, who incrementally "increased in wisdom and stature, and in favour with God and man"[7]—a blended balance of intellectual, physical, spiritual, and social readiness.

On an afternoon a few months ago, Susan and I inventoried our food storage and emergency supplies. At the time, COVID-19 was spreading rapidly, and a series of earthquakes had jolted our home in Utah. We have worked since the earliest days of our marriage to follow prophetic counsel about preparing for unforeseen challenges, so "examining" our state of readiness in the midst of the virus and earthquakes seemed like a good and timely thing to do. We wanted to find out our grades on these unannounced tests.

We learned a great deal. In many areas, our preparatory work was just right. In some other areas, however, improvement was necessary because we had not recognized and addressed particular needs in timely ways.

We also laughed a lot. We discovered, for example, items in a remote closet that had been in our food storage for decades. Frankly, we were afraid to open and inspect some of the containers for fear of unleashing another global pandemic! But you should be happy to know that we properly disposed of the hazardous materials and that health risk to the world was eliminated.

Some Church members opine that emergency plans and supplies, food storage, and 72-hour kits must not be important anymore because the Brethren have not spoken recently and extensively about these and related topics in general conference. But repeated admonitions to prepare have been proclaimed by leaders of the Church for decades. The consistency of prophetic counsel over time creates a powerful concert of clarity and a warning volume far louder than solo performances can ever produce.

Just as challenging times reveal inadequacies in temporal preparedness, so too the maladies of spiritual casualness and complacency inflict their most detrimental effects during difficult trials. We learn, for example, in the parable of the ten virgins that procrastinating preparation leads to unsuccessful proving. Recall how the five foolish virgins failed to prepare appropriately for the examination given to them on the day of the bridegroom's coming.

"They that were foolish took their lamps, and took no oil with them:

"But the wise took oil in their vessels with their lamps. . . .

"And at midnight there was a cry made, Behold, the bridegroom cometh; go ye out to meet him.

"Then all those virgins arose, and trimmed their lamps.

"And the foolish said unto the wise, Give us of your oil; for our lamps are gone out.

"But the wise answered, saying, Not so; lest there be not enough for us and you: but go ye rather to them that sell, and buy for yourselves.

"And while they went to buy, the bridegroom came; and they that were ready went in with him to the marriage: and the door was shut.

"Afterward came also the other virgins, saying, Lord, Lord, open to us."[8]

"But he answered and said, Verily I say unto you, Ye know me not."[9]

At least on this exam, the five foolish virgins proved themselves to be hearers only and not doers of the word.[10]

I have a friend who was a conscientious student in law school. During the course of a semester, Sam invested time every day to review, summarize, and learn from his notes for each course in which he was enrolled. He followed the same pattern for all of his classes at the end of every week and every month. His approach enabled him to learn the law and not merely memorize details. And as final examinations approached, Sam was prepared. In fact, he found the final exam period to be one of the least stressful parts of his legal training. Effective and timely preparation precedes successful proving.

Sam's approach to his legal education highlights one of the Lord's primary patterns for growth and development. "Thus saith the Lord God: I will give unto the children of men line upon line, precept upon precept, here a little and there a little; and blessed are those who hearken unto my precepts, and lend an ear unto my counsel, for they shall learn wisdom; for unto him that receiveth I will give more."[11]

I invite each of us to "consider [our] ways"[12] and "examine [ourselves], whether [we] be in the faith; [and] prove [our] own selves."[13] What have we learned during these recent months of lifestyle adjustments and restrictions? What do we need to improve in our lives spiritually, physically, socially, emotionally, and intellectually? Now is the time to prepare and prove ourselves willing and able to do all things whatsoever the Lord our God shall command us.

Proving and Pressing Forward

I once attended a funeral for a young missionary who was killed in an accident. The missionary's father spoke in the service and described the heartache of an unexpected mortal separation from a beloved child. He forthrightly declared that he personally did not understand the reasons or timing for such an event. But I always will remember this good man also declaring that he knew God knew the reasons and timing for the passing of his child—and that was good enough for him. He told the congregation that he and his family, though sorrowful, would be fine; their testimonies remained firm and steadfast. He concluded his remarks with this declaration: "I want you to know that as far as the gospel of Jesus Christ is concerned, our family is all in. We are all in."

Though the loss of a dear loved one was heart-wrenching and difficult, the members of this valiant family spiritually were prepared to prove that they could learn lessons of eternal importance through the things that they suffered.[14]

Faithfulness is not foolishness or fanaticism. Rather, it is trusting and placing our confidence in Jesus Christ as our Savior, on His name, and in His promises. As we "press forward with a steadfastness in Christ, having a perfect brightness of hope, and a love of God and of all men,"[15] we are blessed with an eternal perspective and vision that stretches far beyond our limited mortal capacity. We will be enabled to "gather together, and stand in holy places"[16] and "be not moved, until the day of the Lord come."[17]

While I was serving as the president of Brigham Young University–Idaho, Elder Jeffrey R. Holland came to the campus in December 1998 to speak in one of our weekly devotionals. Susan and I invited a group of students to meet and visit with Elder Holland before he delivered his message. As our time together was drawing to a close, I asked Elder Holland, "If you could teach these students just one thing, what would it be?"

He answered:

"We are witnessing an ever greater movement toward polarity. The middle-ground options will be removed from us as Latter-day Saints. The middle of the road will be withdrawn.

"If you are treading water in the current of a river, you will go somewhere. You simply will go wherever the current takes you. Going with the stream, following the tide, drifting in the current will not do.

"Choices have to be made. Not making a choice is a choice. Learn to choose now."

Elder Holland's statement about increasing polarization has been proven prophetic by the societal trends and events of the 22 years since he answered my question. Foretelling the widening divergence between the ways of the Lord and of the world, Elder Holland warned that the days of comfortably having one foot in the restored Church and one foot in the world were vanishing quickly. This servant of the Lord was encouraging the young people to choose, prepare, and become devoted disciples of the Savior. He was helping them to prepare and press forward to and through the proving, examining, and trying experiences of their lives.

Promise and Testimony

The process of proving ourselves is a fundamental part of Heavenly Father's great plan of happiness. I promise that as we both prepare and press forward with faith in the Savior, we all can receive the same grade on the ultimate examination of mortality: "Well done, thou good and faithful servant: thou hast been faithful over a few things, I will make thee ruler over many things: enter thou into the joy of thy lord."[18]

I witness that God the Eternal Father is our Father. Jesus Christ is His Only Begotten and living Son, our Savior and Redeemer. Of these truths I joyfully testify in the sacred name of the Lord Jesus Christ, amen.

Notes

1. Abraham 3:25; emphasis added.
2. Psalm 26:2–3; emphasis added.
3. Doctrine and Covenants 98:14; emphasis added.
4. 2 Nephi 2:2.
5. Doctrine and Covenants 88:119; emphasis added.
6. Doctrine and Covenants 38:30–31.
7. Luke 2:52.
8. Matthew 25:3–4, 6–11.
9. Joseph Smith Translation, Matthew 25:12 (in Matthew 25:12, footnote *a*).
10. See James 1:22–25.
11. 2 Nephi 28:30.
12. Haggai 1:5, 7.
13. 2 Corinthians 13:5.
14. See Doctrine and Covenants 105:6.
15. 2 Nephi 31:20.
16. Doctrine and Covenants 101:22.
17. Doctrine and Covenants 87:8.
18. Matthew 25:21.

BECOMING LIKE HIM

ELDER SCOTT D. WHITING
Of the Seventy

To even the careful student of the life and ministry of Jesus Christ, the Savior's admonition to be "even as I am"[1] is daunting and seemingly unattainable. Perhaps you are like me—all too aware of your faults and failings, so you may find it mentally more comfortable to walk a path with no upward incline and little growth. "Surely, this teaching is unrealistic and hyperbole," we rationalize as we comfortably choose the course of least resistance, thereby burning fewer calories of needed change.

But what if becoming "even as [He is]" is not figurative, even in our mortal condition? What if it is, to some degree, attainable in this life and, indeed, a prerequisite to being with Him again? What if "even as I am" is exactly and precisely what is meant by the Savior? Then what? What level of effort would we be willing to give to invite His miraculous power into our lives so that we can change our very nature?

Elder Neal A. Maxwell taught: "As we ponder having been commanded by Jesus to become like Him, we see that our present circumstance is one in which we are not necessarily wicked, but, rather, is one in which we are so half-hearted and so lacking in enthusiasm for His cause—which is our cause, too! We extol but seldom emulate Him."[2] A young minister, Charles M. Sheldon, expressed similar sentiments this way: "Our Christianity loves its ease and comfort too well to take up anything so rough and heavy as a cross."[3]

In fact, all are under the directive to become like Him, just as Jesus Christ became like the Father.[4] As we progress, we become more complete, finished, and fully developed.[5] Such teaching is not based on any one sect's doctrines but comes directly from the Master Himself. It is through this lens that lives should be lived, communications considered, and relationships fostered. Truly, there is no other way to heal the wounds of broken relationships or of a fractured society than for each of us to more fully emulate the Prince of Peace.[6]

Let's consider how to begin a thoughtful, deliberate, and intentional pursuit of becoming as He is by gaining the very attributes of Jesus Christ.

Resolve and Commit

A few years ago, my wife and I stood at the trailhead of Japan's highest mountain, Mount Fuji. As we began our ascent we looked up to the far-distant summit and wondered if we could get there.

As we progressed, fatigue, sore muscles, and the effects of altitude set in. Mentally, it became important for us to focus on just the next step. We would say, "I may not soon make it to the top, but I can do this next step right now." Over time the daunting task ultimately became achievable—step by step.

The first step on this path to becoming like Jesus Christ is to have the desire to do so. Understanding the admonition to be like Him is good, but that understanding needs to be coupled with a yearning to transform ourselves, one step at a time, beyond the natural man.[7] To develop the desire, we must know who Jesus Christ is. We must know something of His character,[8] and we must look for His attributes in scripture, worship services, and other holy places. As we begin to know more of Him, we will see His attributes reflected in others. This will encourage us on our own quest, for if others can attain in some measure His attributes, so can we.

If we are honest with ourselves, the Light of Christ[9] within us whispers that there is distance between where we are in comparison with the desired character of the Savior.[10] Such honesty is vital if we are to progress in becoming like Him. Indeed, honesty is one of His attributes.

Now, those of us who are brave might consider asking a trusted family member, spouse, friend, or spiritual leader what attribute of Jesus Christ we are in need of—and we may need to brace ourselves for the response! Sometimes we see ourselves with distorted fun-house mirrors that show us either much more round or much more lean than we really are.

Trusted friends and family can help us see ourselves more accurately, but even they, as loving and helpful as they would like to be, can see things imperfectly. As a result, it is vital that we also ask our loving Heavenly Father what we are in need of and where we should focus our efforts. He has a perfect view of us and will lovingly show us our weakness.[11] Perhaps you will learn that you need greater patience, humility, charity, love, hope, diligence, or obedience, to name a few.[12]

Not long ago, I had a soul-stretching experience when a loving Church leader made a very direct suggestion that I could use greater measure of a certain attribute. He lovingly cut through any distortion. That night, I shared this experience with my wife. She was mercifully charitable even as she agreed with his suggestion. The Holy Ghost confirmed to me that their counsel was from a loving Heavenly Father.

It may also be helpful to honestly complete the Christlike attribute activity in chapter 6 of *Preach My Gospel.*[13]

Once you have made an honest assessment and resolved to start the hike up the mountain, you will need to repent. President Russell M. Nelson lovingly taught: "When we choose to repent, we choose to change! We allow the Savior to transform us into the best version of ourselves. We choose to grow spiritually and receive joy—the joy of redemption in Him. When we choose to repent, we choose to become more like Jesus Christ."[14]

Becoming as Jesus Christ is will require changing our hearts and minds, indeed, our very character, and doing so is possible only through the saving grace of Jesus Christ.[15]

Identify and Act

Now that you have resolved to change and repent and have sought guidance through praying, pondering honestly, and possibly counseling with others, you will need to select an attribute that will keenly become your focus. You will need to commit to exerting meaningful effort. These attributes won't come cheaply and suddenly, but through His grace they will come incrementally while endeavoring.

Christlike attributes are gifts from a loving Heavenly Father to bless us and those around us. Accordingly, our efforts to obtain these attributes will require heartfelt pleas for His divine assistance. If we seek these gifts to better serve others, He will bless us in our efforts. Selfishly pursuing a gift from God will end in disappointment and frustration.

By focusing deeply on one needed attribute, as you progress in obtaining that attribute, other attributes begin to accrue to you. Can someone who is focusing deeply on charity not increase in love and humility? Can someone who is focusing on obedience not gain greater diligence and hope? Your significant efforts to gain one attribute become the tide that raises all boats in the harbor.

Record and Sustain

It is important for me as I strive to become like Him to record my experiences and what I am learning. As I study with one of His attributes deep in my mind, the scriptures become new as I see examples of this attribute in His teachings, His ministry, and His disciples. My eye also becomes more focused on recognizing the attribute in others. I have observed wonderful individuals both within and without the Church who have attributes that emulate Him. They are powerful examples of how those attributes can be manifest in mere mortals through His loving grace.

In order to see real progress, you will need to put in sustained effort. Much like climbing a mountain requires preparation before and endurance and perseverance during ascent, so too will this journey require real effort and sacrifice. True Christianity, in which we strive to become like our Master, has always required our best efforts.[16]

Now a brief word of caution. The commandment to be like Him is not intended to make you feel guilty, unworthy, or unloved. Our entire mortal experience is about progression, trying, failing, and succeeding. As much as my wife and I may have wished that we could close our eyes and magically transport ourselves to the summit, that is not what life is about.

You are good enough, you are loved, but that does not mean that you are yet complete. There is work to be done in this life and the next. Only with His divine help can we all progress toward becoming like Him.

In these times, when "all things [appear to] be in commotion; and . . . fear [is seemingly] upon all people,"[17] the only antidote, the only remedy, is to strive to be like the Savior,[18] the Redeemer[19] of all mankind, the Light of the World,[20] and to seek after He who declared, "I am the way."[21]

I know that becoming like Him through His divine help and strength *is* achievable step by step. If not so, He would not have given us this commandment.[22] I know this—in part because I see attributes of Him in so many of you. Of these things I testify in the name of Jesus Christ, amen.

Notes

1. 3 Nephi 27:27. For related admonitions from the Savior, see Matthew 5:48 ("Be ye therefore perfect, even as your Father which is in heaven is perfect"); 1 John 2:6 ("He that saith he abideth in him ought himself also so to walk, even as he walked"); Mosiah 3:19 ("For the natural man is an enemy to God, and has been from the fall of Adam, and will be, forever and ever, unless he yields to the enticings of the Holy Spirit, and putteth off the natural man and becometh a saint through the atonement of Christ the Lord, and becometh as a child, submissive, meek, humble, patient, full of love, willing to submit to all things which the Lord seeth fit to inflict upon him, even as a child doth submit to his father"); Alma 5:14 ("And now behold, I ask you, my brethren of the church, have ye spiritually been born of God? Have ye received his image in your countenances?"); 3 Nephi 12:48 ("Therefore I would that ye should be perfect even as I, or your Father who is in heaven is perfect").
2. Neal A. Maxwell, *Even as I Am* (1982), 16.
3. Charles M. Sheldon, *In His Steps* (1979), 185.
4. See Doctrine and Covenants 93:12–17.
5. See Matthew 5:48, footnote b.
6. See Isaiah 9:6; 2 Nephi 19:6.
7. See 1 Corinthians 2:14; Mosiah 3:19.
8. See Matthew 7:23; 25:12; Mosiah 26:24; see also footnotes to each scripture; David A. Bednar, "If Ye Had Known Me," *Ensign* or *Liahona*, Nov. 2016, 102–5.
9. See Doctrine and Covenants 93:2.
10. See Moroni 7:12–19.
11. See Ether 12:27.
12. See *Preach My Gospel: A Guide to Missionary Service*, rev. ed. (2019), chapter 6, "How Do I Develop Christlike Attributes?" References to other attributes of the Savior are scattered among scripture. A few examples include Mosiah 3:19; Alma 7:23; Articles of Faith 1:13.
13. See *Preach My Gospel*, 132.
14. Russell M. Nelson, "We Can Do Better and Be Better," *Ensign* or *Liahona*, May 2019, 67.

15. See Bible Dictionary, "Grace"; Guide to the Scriptures, "Grace," scriptures.ChurchofJesusChrist.org.
16. See Sheldon, *In His Steps*, 246: "If our definition of being a Christian is simply to enjoy the privileges of worship, be generous at no expense to ourselves, have a good, easy time surrounded by pleasant friends and by comfortable things, live respectably and at the same time avoid the world's great stress of sin and trouble because it is too much pain to bear it—if this is our definition of Christianity, surely we are a long way from following [in] the steps of Him who trod the way with groans and tears and sobs of anguish for a lost humanity; who sweat, as it were, great drops of blood, who cried out on the upreared cross, 'My God, my God, why has thou forsaken me?'"
17. Doctrine and Covenants 88:91.
18. See Isaiah 43:3.
19. See Job 19:25.
20. See John 8:12.
21. John 14:6.
22. See 1 Nephi 3:7.

EYES TO SEE

MICHELLE D. CRAIG

First Counselor in the Young Women General Presidency

Seeing God's Hand

I love the Old Testament story of a young man who served the prophet Elisha. Early one morning the young man woke up, went outside, and found the city surrounded by a great army intent on destroying them. He ran to Elisha: "Alas, my master! how shall we do?"

Elisha answered, "Fear not: for they that be with us are more than they that be with them."

Elisha knew the young man needed more than calming reassurance; he needed vision. And so "Elisha prayed, . . . Lord, . . . open his eyes, that he may see. And the Lord opened the eyes of the young man; and he saw: and, behold, the mountain was full of horses and chariots of fire round about Elisha."[1]

There may be times when you, like the servant, find yourself struggling to see how God is working in your life—times when *you* feel under siege—when the trials of mortality bring you to your knees. Wait and trust in God and in His timing, because you can trust His heart with all of yours. But there is a second lesson here. My dear sisters and brothers, you too can pray for the Lord to open your eyes to see things you would not normally see.

Seeing Ourselves as God Sees Us

Perhaps the most important things for us to see clearly are who God is and who we really are—sons and daughters of heavenly parents, with a "divine nature and eternal destiny."[2] Ask God to reveal these truths to you, along with how He feels about you. The more you understand your true identity and purpose, soul deep, the more it will influence everything in your life.

Seeing Others

Understanding how God sees us prepares the way to help us see others as He does. Columnist David Brooks said: "Many of our society's great problems flow from people not feeling seen and known.

. . . [There is a] core . . . trait that we all have to get . . . better at[, and that] is the trait of seeing each other deeply and being deeply seen."[3]

Jesus Christ sees people deeply. He sees individuals, their needs, and who they can become. Where others saw fishermen, sinners, or publicans, Jesus saw disciples; where others saw a man possessed by devils, Jesus looked past the outward distress, acknowledged the man, and healed him.[4]

Even in our busy lives, we can follow the example of Jesus and see individuals—their needs, their faith, their struggle, and who they can become.[5]

As I pray for the Lord to open my eyes to see things I might not normally see, I often ask myself two questions and pay attention to the impressions that come: "What am I doing that I should stop doing?" and "What am I not doing that I should start doing?"[6]

Months ago, during the sacrament, I asked myself these questions and was surprised by the impression that came. "Stop looking at your phone when you are waiting in lines." Looking at my phone in lines had become almost automatic; I found it a good time to multitask, catch up on email, look at headlines, or scroll through a social media feed.

The next morning, I found myself waiting in a long line at the store. I pulled out my phone and then remembered the impression I had received. I put my phone away and looked around. I saw an elderly gentleman in line ahead of me. His cart was empty except for a few cans of cat food. I felt a little awkward but said something *really* clever like, "I can see you have a cat." He said that a storm was coming, and he did not want to be caught without cat food. We visited briefly, and then he turned to me and said, "You know, I haven't told anyone this, but today is my birthday." My heart melted. I wished him a happy birthday and offered a silent prayer of thanks that I had not been on my phone and missed an opportunity to truly see and connect with another person who needed it.

With all of my heart I do not want to be like the priest or the Levite on the road to Jericho—one who looks and passes by.[7] But too often I think I am.

Seeing God's Errand for Me

I recently learned a valuable lesson about seeing deeply from a young woman named Rozlyn.

The story was shared with me by my friend who was devastated when her husband of 20 years moved out. With her children splitting time between parents, the prospect of attending church alone seemed daunting. She recounts:

"In a church where the family is of paramount importance, sitting solo can be painful. That first Sunday I walked in praying no one would speak to me. I was barely holding it together, and tears were on the brink. I sat in my typical spot, hoping no one would notice how empty the bench seemed.

"A young woman in our ward turned and looked at me. I pretended to smile. She smiled back. I could see the concern in her face. I silently pleaded that she wouldn't come to talk to me—I had nothing positive to say and knew I would cry. I looked back down at my lap and avoided eye contact.

"During the next hour, I noticed her looking back at me occasionally. As soon as the meeting ended, she made a beeline for me. 'Hi, Rozlyn,' I whispered. She wrapped me in her arms and said, 'Sister Smith, I can tell today is a bad day for you. I'm so sorry. I love you.' As predicted, the tears came as she hugged me again. But as I walked away, I thought to myself, 'Maybe I can do this after all.'

"That sweet 16-year-old young woman, less than half my age, found me every Sunday for the rest of that year to give me a hug and ask, 'How are you?' It made such a difference in how I felt about coming to church. The truth is I started to *rely* on those hugs. Someone noticed me. Someone knew I was there. Someone cared."

As with all gifts the Father so willingly offers, seeing deeply requires us to *ask Him*—and then *act*. *Ask* to see others as He does—as His true sons and daughters with infinite and divine potential. Then *act* by loving, serving, and affirming their worth and potential as prompted. As this becomes the pattern of our lives, we will find ourselves becoming "true followers of . . . Jesus Christ."[8] Others will be able to trust our hearts with theirs. And in this pattern we will also discover *our own* true identity and purpose.

My friend recalled another experience while sitting in that same empty pew, alone, wondering if 20 years of effort to live the gospel in her home was all for naught. She needed more than calming reassurance; she needed vision. She felt a question pierce her heart: "Why did you do those things? Did you do them for the reward, the praise of others, or the desired outcome?" She hesitated for a moment, searched her heart, and was then able to answer confidently, "I did them because I love the Savior. And I love His gospel." The Lord opened her eyes to help her see. This simple but powerful change of vision helped her continue to press on with faith in Christ, despite her circumstances.

I witness that Jesus Christ loves us and can give us eyes to see—*even* when it's hard, *even* when we're tired, *even* when we're lonely, and *even* when the outcomes are not as we hoped. Through His grace, He will bless us and increase our capacity. Through the power of the Holy Ghost, Christ will enable us to *see* ourselves and *see* others as He does. With His help, we can discern what is most needful. We can begin to see the hand of the Lord working in and through the ordinary details of our lives—we will see deeply.

And then, in that great day "when he shall appear we shall be like him, for *we* shall *see him* as he is; that we may have this hope"[9] is my prayer in the name of Jesus Christ, amen.

Notes

1. 2 Kings 6:15–17.
2. Young Women theme, ChurchofJesusChrist.org.
3. David Brooks, "Finding the Road to Character" (Brigham Young University forum address, Oct. 22, 2019), speeches.byu.edu.
4. See Mark 5:1–15.
5. "It is a serious thing to live in a society of possible gods and goddesses, to remember that the dullest . . . most uninteresting person you can talk to may one day be a creature which, if you saw it now, you would be strongly tempted to worship. . . . There are no ordinary people" (C. S. Lewis, *The Weight of Glory* [2001], 45–46).
6. Kim B. Clark, "Encircled about with Fire" (Seminaries and Institutes of Religion satellite broadcast, Aug. 4, 2015), ChurchofJesusChrist.org.
7. See Luke 10:30–32.
8. Moroni 7:48.
9. Moroni 7:48; emphasis added.

HEARTS KNIT IN RIGHTEOUSNESS AND UNITY

ELDER QUENTIN L. COOK
Of the Quorum of the Twelve Apostles

Righteousness and unity are profoundly significant.[1] When people love God with all their hearts and righteously strive to become like Him, there is less strife and contention in society. There is more unity. I love a true account that exemplifies this.

As a young man not of our faith, General Thomas L. Kane assisted and defended the Saints as they were required to flee Nauvoo. He was an advocate for the Church for many years.[2]

In 1872, General Kane, his talented wife, Elizabeth Wood Kane, and their two sons traveled from their home in Pennsylvania to Salt Lake City. They accompanied Brigham Young and his associates on a trek south to St. George, Utah. Elizabeth approached her first visit to Utah with reservations about the women. She was surprised by some of the things she learned. For instance, she found that any career by which a woman could earn a living was open to them in Utah.[3] She also found Church members were kind and understanding with respect to Native Americans.[4]

During the trip they stayed in Fillmore at the home of Thomas R. and Matilda Robison King.[5]

Elizabeth wrote that as Matilda was preparing a meal for President Young and his company, five American Indians came into the room. Although uninvited, it was clear they expected to join the company. Sister King spoke to them "in their dialect." They sat down with their blankets with a pleasant look on their faces. Elizabeth asked one of the King children, "What did your mother say to those men?"

Matilda's son's reply was, "She said 'These strangers came first, and I have only cooked enough for them; but your meal is on the fire cooking now, and I will call you as soon as it is ready.'"

Elizabeth asked, "Will she really do that, or just give them scraps at the kitchen-door?"[6]

Matilda's son answered, "Mother will serve them just as she does you, and give them a place at her table."

And so she did, and "they ate with perfect propriety." Elizabeth explained that this hostess rose 100 percent in her opinion.[7] Unity is enhanced when people are treated with dignity and respect, even though they are different in outward characteristics.

As leaders, we are not under the illusion that in the past all relationships were perfect, all conduct was Christlike, or all decisions were just. However, our faith teaches that we are all children of our Father in Heaven, and we worship Him and His Son, Jesus Christ, who is our Savior. Our desire is that our hearts and minds will be knit in righteousness and unity and that we will be one with Them.[8]

Righteousness is a broad, comprehensive term but most certainly includes living God's commandments.[9] It qualifies us for the sacred ordinances that constitute the covenant path and blesses us to have the Spirit give direction to our lives.[10]

Being righteous is not dependent on each of us having every blessing in our lives at this time. We may not be married or blessed with children or have other desired blessings now. But the Lord has promised that the righteous who are faithful "may dwell with God in a state of never-ending happiness."[11]

Unity is also a broad, comprehensive term but most certainly exemplifies the first and second great commandments to love God and love our fellowmen.[12] It denotes a Zion people whose hearts and minds are "knit together in unity."[13]

The context for my message is the contrast and lessons from sacred scriptures.

It has been 200 years since the Father and His Son first appeared and commenced the Restoration of the gospel of Jesus Christ in 1820. The account in 4 Nephi in the Book of Mormon includes a similar 200-year period after the Savior appeared and established His Church in ancient America.

The historical record we read in 4 Nephi describes a people where there were no envyings, strifes, tumults, lyings, murders, or any manner of lasciviousness. Because of this righteousness, the record states, "surely there could not be a happier people among all the people who had been created by the hand of God."[14]

With respect to unity, 4 Nephi reads, "There was no contention in the land, because of the love of God which did dwell in the hearts of the people."[15]

Unfortunately, 4 Nephi then describes a dramatic change that began in the "two hundred and first year,"[16] when iniquity and division destroyed righteousness and unity. The depths of depravity that then occurred were subsequently so evil that ultimately the great prophet Mormon laments to his son Moroni:

"But O my son, how can a people like this, whose delight is in so much abomination—

"How can we expect that God will stay his hand in judgment against us?"[17]

In this dispensation, although we live in a special time, the world has not been blessed with the righteousness and unity described in 4 Nephi. Indeed, we live in a moment of particularly strong divisions. However, the millions who have accepted the gospel of Jesus Christ have committed themselves to achieving both righteousness and unity. We are all aware that we can do better, and that is our challenge in this day. We can be a force to lift and bless society as a whole. At this 200-year hinge point in our Church history, let us commit ourselves as members of the Lord's Church to live righteously and be united as never before. President Russell M. Nelson has asked us "to demonstrate greater civility, racial and ethnic harmony and mutual respect."[18] This means loving each other and God and accepting everyone as brothers and sisters and truly being a Zion people.

With our all-inclusive doctrine, we can be an oasis of unity and celebrate diversity. Unity and diversity are not opposites. We can achieve greater unity as we foster an atmosphere of inclusion and respect for diversity. During the period I served in the San Francisco California Stake presidency, we had Spanish-, Tongan-, Samoan-, Tagalog-, and Mandarin-language-speaking congregations. Our

English-speaking wards were composed of people from many racial and cultural backgrounds. There was love, righteousness, and unity.

Wards and branches in The Church of Jesus Christ of Latter-day Saints are determined by geography or language,[19] not by race or culture. Race is not identified on membership records.

Early in the Book of Mormon, approximately 550 years before the birth of Christ, we are taught the fundamental commandment regarding the relationship between Father in Heaven's children. All are to keep the Lord's commandments, and all are invited to partake of the Lord's goodness; "and he denieth none that come unto him, black and white, bond and free, male and female; and he remembereth the heathen; and all are alike unto God, both Jew and Gentile."[20]

The Savior's ministry and message have consistently declared all races and colors are children of God. We are all brothers and sisters. In our doctrine we believe that in the host country for the Restoration, the United States, the U.S. Constitution[21] and related documents,[22] written by imperfect men, were inspired by God to bless all people. As we read in the Doctrine and Covenants, these documents were "established, and should be maintained for the rights and protection *of all flesh,* according to just and holy principles."[23] Two of these principles were agency and accountability for one's own sins. The Lord declared:

"Therefore, it is not right that any man should be in bondage one to another.

"And for this purpose have I established the Constitution of this land, by the hands of wise men whom I raised up unto this very purpose, and redeemed the land by the shedding of blood."[24]

This revelation was received in 1833 when the Saints in Missouri were suffering great persecution. The heading to Doctrine and Covenants section 101 reads in part: "Mobs had driven them from their homes in Jackson County. . . . Threats of death against [members] of the Church were many."[25]

This was a time of tension on several fronts. Many Missourians considered Native Americans a relentless enemy and wanted them removed from the land. In addition, many of the Missouri settlers were slave owners and felt threatened by those who were opposed to slavery.

In contrast, our doctrine respected the Native Americans, and our desire was to teach them the gospel of Jesus Christ. With respect to slavery, our scriptures had made it clear that no man should be in bondage to another.[26]

Ultimately, the Saints were violently driven out of Missouri[27] and then forced to move to the West.[28] The Saints prospered and found the peace that accompanies righteousness, unity, and living the gospel of Jesus Christ.

I rejoice in the Savior's Intercessory Prayer recorded in the Gospel of John. The Savior acknowledged that the Father had sent Him and that He, the Savior, had finished the work He was sent to do. He prayed for His disciples and for those who would believe in Christ: "That they all may be one; as thou, Father, art in me, and I in thee, that they also may be one in us."[29] Oneness is what Christ prayed for prior to His betrayal and Crucifixion.

In the first year after the Restoration of the gospel of Jesus Christ, recorded in section 38 of the Doctrine and Covenants, the Lord speaks of wars and wickedness and declares, "I say unto you, be one; and if ye are not one ye are not mine."[30]

Our Church culture comes from the gospel of Jesus Christ. The Epistle of the Apostle Paul to the Romans is profound.[31] The early Church in Rome was composed of Jews and Gentiles. These early Jews had a Judaic culture and had "won their emancipation, and began to multiply and flourish."[32]

The Gentiles in Rome had a culture with a significant Hellenistic influence, which the Apostle Paul understood well because of his experiences at Athens and Corinth.

Paul sets forth the gospel of Jesus Christ in a comprehensive fashion. He chronicles pertinent aspects of both Judaic and Gentile culture[33] that conflict with the true gospel of Jesus Christ. He essentially asks each of them to leave behind cultural impediments from their beliefs and culture that are not consistent with the gospel of

Jesus Christ. Paul admonishes the Jews and the Gentiles to keep the commandments and love one another and affirms that righteousness leads to salvation.[34]

The culture of the gospel of Jesus Christ is not a Gentile culture or a Judaic culture. It is not determined by the color of one's skin or where one lives. While we rejoice in distinctive cultures, we should leave behind aspects of those cultures that conflict with the gospel of Jesus Christ. Our members and new converts often come from diverse racial and cultural backgrounds. If we are to follow President Nelson's admonition to gather scattered Israel, we will find we are as different as the Jews and Gentiles were in Paul's time. Yet we can be united in our love of and faith in Jesus Christ. Paul's Epistle to the Romans establishes the principle that we follow the culture and doctrine of the gospel of Jesus Christ. It is the model for us even today.[35] The ordinances of the temple unite us in special ways and allow us to be one in every eternally significant way.

We honor our pioneer members across the world not because they were perfect but because they overcame hardships, made sacrifices, aspired to be Christlike, and were striving to build faith and be one with the Savior. Their oneness with the Savior made them one with each other. This principle is true for you and me today.

The clarion call to members of The Church of Jesus Christ of Latter-day Saints is to strive to be a Zion people who are of one heart and one mind and dwell in righteousness.[36]

It is my prayer that we will be righteous and united and completely focused on serving and worshipping our Savior, Jesus Christ, of whom I testify. In the name of Jesus Christ, amen.

Notes

1. See Doctrine and Covenants 38:27.
2. Thomas Kane's service in behalf of the members has consistently been portrayed "as an act of selfless sacrifice by a young idealist who witnessed the injustices inflicted upon a persecuted religious minority by a cruel and hostile majority" (introduction to Elizabeth Wood Kane, *Twelve Mormon Homes Visited in Succession on a Journey through Utah to Arizona*, ed. Everett L. Cooley [1974], viii).
3. See Kane, *Twelve Mormon Homes*, 5.
4. See Kane, *Twelve Mormon Homes*, 40.
5. See Lowell C. (Ben) Bennion and Thomas R. Carter, "Touring Polygamous Utah with Elizabeth W. Kane, Winter 1872–1873," *BYU Studies*, vol. 48, no. 4 (2009), 162.

6. Apparently, Elizabeth assumed most Americans at that time would have given the American Indians just scraps and treated them differently from their other guests.
7. See Kane, *Twelve Mormon Homes*, 64–65. It is noteworthy that many Native Americans, including several chiefs, became members of the Church. See also John Alton Peterson, *Utah's Black Hawk War* (1998) 61; Scott R. Christensen, *Sagwitch: Shoshone Chieftain, Mormon Elder, 1822–1887* (1999), 190–95.
8. In this dispensation "the righteous shall be gathered out from among all nations, and shall come to Zion, singing with songs of everlasting joy" (Doctrine and Covenants 45:71).
9. See Doctrine and Covenants 105:3–5. Scriptures have singled out caring for the poor and needy as being a necessary element of righteousness.
10. See Alma 36:30; see also 1 Nephi 2:20; Mosiah 1:7. The last part of Alma 36:30 reads, "Inasmuch as ye will not keep the commandments of God ye shall be cut off from his presence. Now this is according to his word."
11. Mosiah 2:41. President Lorenzo Snow (1814–1901) taught: "There is no Latter-day Saint who dies after having lived a faithful life who will lose anything because of having failed to do certain things when opportunities were not furnished him or her. In other words, if a young man or a young woman has no opportunity of getting married, and they live faithful lives up to the time of their death, they will have all the blessings, exaltation and glory that any man or woman will have who had this opportunity and improved it. That is sure and positive" (*Teachings of Presidents of the Church: Lorenzo Snow* [2012], 130). See also Richard G. Scott, "The Joy of Living the Great Plan of Happiness," *Ensign*, Nov. 1996, 75.
12. See 1 John 5:2.
13. Mosiah 18:21; see also Moses 7:18.
14. 4 Nephi 1:16.
15. 4 Nephi 1:15.
16. 4 Nephi 1:24.
17. Moroni 9:13–14.
18. Russell M. Nelson, in "First Presidency and NAACP Leaders Call for Greater Civility, Racial Harmony," May 17, 2018, newsroom.ChurchofJesusChrist.org; see also "President Nelson Remarks at Worldwide Priesthood Celebration," June 1, 2018, newsroom.ChurchofJesusChrist.org.
19. Doctrine and Covenants 90:11 reads, "Every man shall hear the fulness of the gospel . . . in his own language." Accordingly, language congregations are usually approved.
20. 2 Nephi 26:33.
21. See Constitution of the United States.
22. See United States Declaration of Independence (1776); Constitution of the United States, Amendments I–X (Bill of Rights), National Archives website, archives.gov/founding-docs.
23. Doctrine and Covenants 101:77; emphasis added.
24. Doctrine and Covenants 101:79–80.
25. Doctrine and Covenants 101, section heading.
26. See *Saints: The Story of the Church of Jesus Christ in the Latter Days*, vol. 1, *The Standard of Truth, 1815–1846* (2018), 172–74; James B. Allen and Glen M. Leonard, *The Story of the Latter-day Saints*, 2nd ed. (1992), 93–94; Ronald W. Walker, "Seeking the 'Remnant': The Native American during the Joseph Smith Period," *Journal of Mormon History*, vol. 19, no. 1 (Spring 1993), 14–16.
27. See *Saints*, 1:359–83; William G. Hartley, "The Saints' Forced Exodus from Missouri, 1839," in Richard Neitzel Holzapfel and Kent P. Jackson, eds., *Joseph Smith, the Prophet and Seer* (2010), 347–89; Alexander L. Baugh, "The Mormons Must Be Treated as Enemies," in Susan Easton Black and Andrew C. Skinner, eds., *Joseph: Exploring the Life and Ministry of the Prophet* (2005), 284–95.
28. *See Saints: The Story of the Church of Jesus Christ in the Latter Days*, vol. 2, *No Unhallowed Hand, 1846–1893* (2020), 3–68; Richard E. Bennett, *We'll Find the Place: The Mormon Exodus, 1846–1848* (1997); William W. Slaughter and Michael Landon, *Trail of Hope: The Story of the Mormon Trail* (1997).
29. John 17:21.
30. Doctrine and Covenants 38:27.
31. The Epistle to the Romans is comprehensive in declaring doctrine. Romans contains the only mention of the Atonement in the New Testament.

32. Frederic W. Farrar, *The Life and Work of St. Paul* (1898), 446.
33. See Farrar, *The Life and Work of St. Paul*, 450.
34. See Romans 13.
35. See Dallin H. Oaks, "The Gospel Culture," *Ensign*, Mar. 2012, 42–45; *Liahona*, Mar. 2012, 22–25; see also Richard G. Scott, "Removing Barriers to Happiness," *Ensign*, May 1998, 85–87.
36. See Moses 7:18.

RECOMMENDED TO THE LORD

ELDER RONALD A. RASBAND

Of the Quorum of the Twelve Apostles

Good morning, brothers and sisters. As a disciple of our Savior, Jesus Christ, I have been looking forward to gathering virtually from all corners of the world for this conference.

This has been a most unusual year. For me it began with an assignment from the First Presidency to dedicate a holy temple to the Lord in Durban, South Africa. I will never forget the grandeur of the building. But more than the setting, I will always treasure the dignity of the people who were so well prepared to enter that sacred edifice. They came ready to partake of one of the crowning blessings of the Restoration: the dedication of a house of the Lord. They came with hearts filled with love for Him and His Atonement. They came filled with thanks to our Father in Heaven for providing sacred ordinances that would lead to exaltation. They came worthy.

Temples, no matter where they are, rise above the ways of the world. Every Latter-day Saint temple in the world—all 168 of them—stand as testaments to our faith in eternal life and the joy of spending it with our families and our Heavenly Father. Attending the temple increases our understanding of the Godhead and the everlasting gospel, our commitment to live and teach truth, and our willingness to follow the example of our Lord and Savior, Jesus Christ.

On the outside of every temple in the Church are the fitting words "Holiness to the Lord." The temple is the Lord's house and a sanctuary from the world. His Spirit envelops those who worship within those sacred walls. He sets the standards by which we enter as His guests.

My father-in-law, Blaine Twitchell, one of the best men I have ever known, taught me a great lesson. Sister Rasband and I went to visit him when he was nearing the end of his mortal journey. As we entered his room, his bishop was just leaving. As we greeted the bishop, I thought, "What a nice bishop. He's here doing his ministering to a faithful member of his ward."

I mentioned to Blaine, "Wasn't that nice of the bishop to come visit."

Blaine looked at me and responded, "It was far more than that. I asked for the bishop to come because I wanted my temple recommend interview. I want to go *recommended to the Lord.*" And he did!

That phrase, "recommended to the Lord," has stayed with me. It has put a whole new perspective on being interviewed regularly by our Church leaders. So important is a temple recommend that in the early Church, until 1891, each temple recommend was endorsed by the President of the Church.[1]

Whether for youth or adults, your temple recommend interview is not about do's and don'ts. A recommend is not a checklist, a hall pass, or a ticket for special seating. It has a much higher and holier purpose. To qualify for the honor of a temple recommend, you must live in harmony with the teachings of The Church of Jesus Christ of Latter-day Saints.

In your interview you have the opportunity to search your soul about your personal faith in Jesus Christ and His Atonement. You have the blessing to express your testimony of the restored gospel; your willingness to sustain those whom the Lord has called to lead His Church; your faith in the doctrine of the gospel; your fulfillment of family responsibilities; and your qualities of honesty, chastity, fidelity, obedience, and observance of the Word of Wisdom, the law of tithing, and the sanctity of the Sabbath day. Those are bedrock principles of a life devoted to Jesus Christ and His work.

Your temple recommend reflects a deep, spiritual intent that you are striving to live the laws of the Lord and love what He loves: humility, meekness, steadfastness, charity, courage, compassion, forgiveness, and obedience. And you commit yourself to those standards when you sign your name to that sacred document.

Your temple recommend opens the gates of heaven for you and others with rites and ordinances of eternal significance, including baptisms, endowments, marriages, and sealings.

To be "recommended to the Lord" is to be reminded of what is expected of a covenant-keeping Latter-day Saint. My father-in-law, Blaine, saw it as invaluable preparation for the day when he would humbly stand before the Lord.

Consider when Moses climbed Mount Horeb and the Lord Jehovah appeared to him in a burning bush. God told him, "Put off thy shoes from off thy feet, for the place whereon thou standest is holy ground."[2]

Putting off our shoes at the door of the temple is letting go of worldly desires or pleasures that distract us from spiritual growth, setting aside those things which sidetrack our precious mortality, rising above contentious behavior, and seeking time to be holy.

By divine design, our physical body is a creation of God, a temple for our spirit, and should be treated with reverence. So true are the words of the Primary song: "My body is a temple [that] needs the greatest care."[3] When the Lord appeared to the Nephites, He commanded, "Be sanctified by the reception of the Holy Ghost, that ye may stand spotless before me."[4] "What manner of men ought ye to be?" asked the Lord and then answered, "Even as I am."[5] To be "recommended to the Lord," we strive to be like Him.

I remember hearing President Howard W. Hunter in his first general conference address as the 14th President of the Church. He said: "It is the deepest desire of my heart to have every member of the Church worthy to enter the temple. It would please the Lord if every adult member would be worthy of—and carry—a current temple recommend."[6] I would add that a limited-use recommend will set a clear path for our precious youth.

President Russell M. Nelson recalled President Hunter's words: "On that day, June 6, 1994, the temple recommend that we carry became a different object in my wallet. Before that, it was a means to an end. It was the means to allow me to enter a sacred house of the Lord; but after he made that declaration, that became an end in itself. It became my badge of obedience to a prophet of God."[7]

If you have yet to receive a recommend or if your recommend has lapsed, line up at the door of the bishop just as the early Saints lined up at the door of the Nauvoo Temple in 1846.[8] My ancestors were among those faithful. They were abandoning their beautiful city and going west, but they knew that there were sacred experiences awaiting them in the temple. Wrote Sarah Rich from the rugged trail in Iowa, "If it had not been for the faith and knowledge that was bestowed upon us in that temple . . . , our journey would have been like . . . taking a leap in the dark."[9] That is what we are missing if we are going through this life alone without the inspiration and peace promised in the temple.

Begin the process now to become "recommended to the Lord" so that His Spirit will be with you in abundance and His standards will bring you "peace of conscience."[10]

Your youth leaders, elders quorum president, Relief Society president, and ministering brothers and sisters will help you prepare, and your bishop or branch president lovingly will guide you.

We have been experiencing a time when temples have been closed or limited in use. For President Nelson and those of us who serve at his side, the inspired decision to close the temples was "painful" and "wracked with worry." President Nelson found himself asking, "What would I say to the Prophet Joseph Smith? What would I say to Brigham Young, Wilford Woodruff and the other Presidents, on up to President Thomas S. Monson?"[11]

Now, we gradually and gratefully are reopening temples for sealings and endowments on a limited scale.

Being worthy to attend the temple, however, has not been suspended. Let me emphasize, whether you have access to a temple or not, you need a current temple recommend to stay firmly on the covenant path.

Late last year Sister Rasband and I were on assignment in New Zealand speaking with a large group of young single adults. They had no easy access to a temple; the one in Hamilton was being renovated, and they were still awaiting the groundbreaking for the temple in Auckland. However, I felt prompted to encourage them to renew or receive temple recommends.

Even though they could not present them at the temple, they

would be presenting themselves before the Lord pure and prepared to serve Him. Being worthy to hold a current temple recommend is both a protection from the adversary, because you have made a firm commitment to the Lord about your life, and a promise that the Spirit will be with you.

We do temple work when we search for our ancestors and submit their names for ordinances. While our temples have been closed, we have still been able to research our families. With the Spirit of God in our hearts, we are, by proxy, standing in for them to be "recommended to the Lord."

When I was serving as the Executive Director of the Temple Department, I heard President Gordon B. Hinckley refer to this scripture spoken by the Lord about the Nauvoo Temple: "Let the work of my temple, and all the works which I have appointed unto you, be continued on and not cease; and let your diligence, and your perseverance, and patience, and your works be redoubled, and you shall in nowise lose your reward, saith the Lord of Hosts."[12]

Our work in the temple is tied to our eternal reward. Recently we have been put to the test. The Lord has called us to work in the temples with "diligence, . . . perseverance, and patience."[13] Being "recommended to the Lord" requires those qualities. We must be diligent in living the commandments, persevere in our attention to our temple covenants, and be grateful for what the Lord continues to teach about them and be patient as we wait for temples to reopen in their fulness.

When the Lord calls for us to "redouble" our efforts, He is asking that we increase in righteousness. For example, we may expand our study of the scriptures, our family history research, and our prayers of faith that we may share our love for the Lord's house with those preparing to receive a temple recommend, our family members in particular.

I promise you as an Apostle of the Lord Jesus Christ that as you strive to redouble your righteous efforts, you will feel renewed in your devotion to God the Father and Jesus Christ, you will feel an abundance of the Holy Ghost guiding you, you will be grateful for your sacred covenants, and you will feel peace knowing you are "recommended to the Lord." In the name of Jesus Christ, amen.

Notes

1. See James R. Clark, comp., *Messages of the First Presidency of The Church of Jesus Christ of Latter-day Saints, 1833–1964*, 6 vols. (1965–75), 3:229.
2. Exodus 3:5.
3. "My Body Is a Temple," *The Children Sing* (1951), no. 99.
4. 3 Nephi 27:20.
5. 3 Nephi 27:27.
6. *Teachings of Presidents of the Church: Howard W. Hunter* (2015), 180.
7. *Teachings of Russell M. Nelson* (2018), 373.
8. See *Saints: The Story of the Church of Jesus Christ in the Latter Days*, vol. 1, *The Standard of Truth, 1815–1846* (2018), 582–83.
9. Sarah P. Rich, Autobiography, 1885–1890, Church History Library, Salt Lake City, 66.
10. Mosiah 4:3.
11. Sarah Jane Weaver, "President Nelson Talks about the 'Painful' Decision to Close Temples amid COVID-19," *Church News*, July 27, 2020, thechurchnews.com.
12. Doctrine and Covenants 127:4.
13. Doctrine and Covenants 127:4.

LOVE YOUR ENEMIES

PRESIDENT DALLIN H. OAKS
First Counselor in the First Presidency

The Lord's teachings are for eternity and for all of God's children. In this message I will give some examples from the United States, but the principles I teach are applicable everywhere.

We live in a time of anger and hatred in political relationships and policies. We felt it this summer when some went beyond peaceful protests and engaged in destructive behavior. We feel it in some current campaigns for public offices. Unfortunately, some of this has even spilled over into political statements and unkind references in our Church meetings.

In a democratic government we will always have differences over proposed candidates and policies. However, as followers of Christ we must forgo the anger and hatred with which political choices are debated or denounced in many settings.

Here is one of our Savior's teachings, probably well known but rarely practiced:

"Ye have heard that it hath been said, Thou shalt love thy neighbour, and hate thine enemy.

"But I say unto you, Love your enemies, bless them that curse you, do good to them that hate you, and pray for them which despitefully use you, and persecute you" (Matthew 5:43–44).[1]

For generations, Jews had been taught to hate their enemies, and they were then suffering under the domination and cruelties of Roman occupation. Yet Jesus taught them, "Love your enemies" and "do good to them that . . . despitefully use you."

What revolutionary teachings for personal and political relationships! But that is still what our Savior commands. In the Book of Mormon we read, "For verily, verily I say unto you, he that hath the spirit of contention is not of me, but is of the devil, who is the father of contention, and he stirreth up the hearts of men to contend with anger, one with another" (3 Nephi 11:29).

Loving our enemies and our adversaries is not easy. "Most of us have not reached that stage of . . . love and forgiveness," President Gordon B. Hinckley observed, adding, "It requires a self-discipline almost greater than we are capable of."[2] But it must be essential, for it is part of the Savior's two great commandments to "love the Lord thy God" and to "love thy neighbour as thyself" (Matthew 22:37, 39). And it must be possible, for He also taught, "Ask, and it shall be given you; seek, and ye shall find" (Matthew 7:7).[3]

How do we keep these divine commandments in a world where we are also subject to the laws of man? Fortunately, we have the Savior's own example of how to balance His eternal laws with the practicalities of man-made laws. When adversaries sought to trap Him with a question about whether Jews should pay taxes to Rome, He pointed to the image of Caesar on their coins and declared, "Render therefore unto Caesar the things which be Caesar's, and unto God the things which be God's" (Luke 20:25).[4]

So, we are to follow the laws of men (render unto Caesar) to live peacefully under civil authority, and we follow the laws of God toward our eternal destination. But how do we do this—especially how do we learn to love our adversaries and our enemies?

The Savior's teaching not to "contend with anger" is a good first step. The devil is the father of contention, and it is he who tempts men to contend with anger. He promotes enmity and hateful relationships among individuals and within groups. President Thomas S. Monson taught that anger is "Satan's tool," for "to be angry is to yield to the influence of Satan. No one can *make* us angry. It is our choice."[5] Anger is the way to division and enmity. We move toward loving our adversaries when we avoid anger and hostility toward those with whom we disagree. It also helps if we are even willing to learn from them.

Among other ways to develop the power to love others is the simple method described in a long-ago musical. When we are trying to understand and relate to people of a different culture, we should try getting to know them. In countless circumstances, strangers' suspicion or even hostility give way to friendship or even love when personal contacts produce understanding and mutual respect.[6]

An even greater help in learning to love our adversaries and our enemies is to seek to understand the power of love. Here are three of many prophetic teachings about this.

The Prophet Joseph Smith taught that "it is a time-honored adage that love begets love. Let us pour forth love—show forth our kindness unto all mankind."[7]

President Howard W. Hunter taught: "The world in which we live would benefit greatly if men and women everywhere would exercise the pure love of Christ, which is kind, meek, and lowly. It is without envy or pride. . . . It seeks nothing in return. . . . It has no place for bigotry, hatred, or violence. . . . It encourages diverse people to live together in Christian love regardless of religious belief, race, nationality, financial standing, education, or culture."[8]

And President Russell M. Nelson has urged us to "expand our circle of love to embrace the whole human family."[9]

An essential part of loving our enemies is to render unto Caesar by keeping the laws of our various countries. Though Jesus's teachings were revolutionary, He did not teach revolution or lawbreaking. He taught a better way. Modern revelation teaches the same:

"Let no man break the laws of the land, for he that keepeth the laws of God hath no need to break the laws of the land.

"Wherefore, be subject to the powers that be" (Doctrine and Covenants 58:21–22).

And our article of faith, written by the Prophet Joseph Smith after the early Saints had suffered severe persecution from Missouri officials, declares, "We believe in being subject to kings, presidents, rulers, and magistrates, in obeying, honoring, and sustaining the law" (Articles of Faith 1:12).

This does not mean that we agree with all that is done with the force of law. It means that we obey the current law and use peaceful means to change it. It also means that we peacefully accept the results of elections. We will not participate in the violence threatened by those disappointed with the outcome.[10] In a democratic society we always have the opportunity and the duty to persist peacefully until the next election.

The Savior's teaching to love our enemies is based on the reality that all mortals are beloved children of God. That eternal principle and some basic principles of law were tested in the recent protests in many American cities.

At one extreme, some seem to have forgotten that the First Amendment to the United States Constitution guarantees the "right of the people peaceably to assemble, and to petition the Government for a redress of grievances." That is the authorized way to raise public awareness and to focus on injustices in the content or administration of the laws. And there have been injustices. In public actions and in our personal attitudes, we have had racism and related grievances. In a persuasive personal essay, the Reverend Theresa A. Dear of the National Association for the Advancement of Colored People (NAACP) has reminded us that "racism thrives on hatred, oppression, collusion, passivity, indifference and silence."[11] As citizens and as members of The Church of Jesus Christ of Latter-day Saints, we must do better to help root out racism.

At the other extreme, a minority of participants and supporters of these protests and the illegal acts that followed them seem to have forgotten that the protests protected by the Constitution are *peaceful* protests. Protesters have no right to destroy, deface, or steal property or to undermine the government's legitimate police powers. The Constitution and laws contain no invitation to revolution or anarchy. All of us—police, protesters, supporters, and spectators—should understand the limits of our rights and the importance of our duties to stay within the boundaries of existing law. Abraham Lincoln was right when he said, "There is no grievance that is a fit object of redress by mob law."[12] Redress of grievances by mobs is redress by illegal means. That is anarchy, a condition that has no effective governance and no formal police, which undermines rather than protects individual rights.

One reason the recent protests in the United States were shocking to so many was that the hostilities and illegalities felt among different ethnicities in other nations should not be felt in the United States. This country should be better in eliminating racism not only against Black Americans, who were most visible in the recent protests, but also against Latinos, Asians, and other groups. This nation's history of racism is not a happy one, and we must do better.

The United States was founded by immigrants of different nationalities and different ethnicities. Its unifying purpose was not to establish a particular religion or to perpetuate any of the diverse cultures or tribal loyalties of the old countries. Our founding generation sought to be unified by a new constitution and laws. That is not to say that our unifying documents or the then-current understanding of their meanings were perfect. The history of the first two centuries of the United States showed the need for many refinements, such as voting rights for women and, particularly, the abolition of slavery, including laws to ensure that those who had been enslaved would have all the conditions of freedom.

Two Yale University scholars recently reminded us:

"For all its flaws, the United States is uniquely equipped to unite a diverse and divided society. . . .

". . . Its citizens don't have to choose between a national identity and multiculturalism. Americans can have both. But the key is constitutional patriotism. We have to remain united by and through the Constitution, regardless of our ideological disagreements."[13]

Many years ago, a British foreign secretary gave this great counsel in a debate in the House of Commons: "We have no eternal *allies* and we have no perpetual *enemies.* Our *interests* are eternal and perpetual, and these interests it is our duty to follow."[14]

That is a good *secular* reason for following "eternal and perpetual" interests in political matters. In addition, the doctrine of the Lord's Church teaches us another eternal interest to guide us: the teachings of our Savior, who inspired the Constitution of the United States and the basic laws of many of our countries. Loyalty to established law instead of temporary "allies" is the best way to love our adversaries and our enemies as we seek unity in diversity.

Knowing that we are all children of God gives us a divine vision of the worth of all others and the will and ability to rise above prejudice and racism. As I have lived for many years in different places in this nation, the Lord has taught me that it is possible to obey and seek to improve our nation's laws and also to love our adversaries and our enemies. While not easy, it is possible with the help of our Lord, Jesus Christ. He gave this command to love, and He promises His help as we seek to obey it. I testify that we are loved and will be helped by our Heavenly Father and His Son, Jesus Christ. In the name of Jesus Christ, amen.

Notes

1. See also Luke 6:27–28, 30.
2. Gordon B. Hinckley, "The Healing Power of Christ," *Ensign*, Nov. 1988, 59; see also *Teachings of Gordon B. Hinckley* (1997), 230.
3. See also Doctrine and Covenants 6:5.
4. See also Matthew 22:21; Mark 12:17.
5. Thomas S. Monson, "School Thy Feelings, O My Brother," *Ensign* or *Liahona*, Nov. 2009, 68.
6. See Becky and Bennett Borden, "Moving Closer: Loving as the Savior Did," *Ensign*, Sept. 2020, 24–27.
7. Joseph Smith, in *History of the Church*, 5:517. Similarly, Martin Luther King Jr. (1929–68) said: "Returning violence for violence multiplies violence, adding deeper darkness to a night already devoid of stars. Darkness cannot drive out darkness: only light can do that. Hate cannot drive out hate: only love can do that" (*Where Do We Go from Here: Chaos or Community?* [2010], 64–65).
8. *Teachings of Presidents of the Church: Howard W. Hunter* (2015), 263.
9. Russell M. Nelson, "Blessed Are the Peacemakers," *Ensign* or *Liahona*, Nov. 2002, 41; see also *Teachings of Russell M. Nelson* (2018), 83.
10. See "A House Divided," *Economist*, Sept. 5, 2020, 17–20.
11. Theresa A. Dear, "America's Tipping Point: 7 Ways to Dismantle Racism," *Deseret News*, June 7, 2020, A1.
12. Abraham Lincoln, address at the Young Men's Lyceum, Springfield, Illinois, Jan. 27, 1838, in John Bartlett, *Bartlett's Familiar Quotations*, 18th ed. (2012), 444.
13. Amy Chua and Jed Rubenfeld, "The Threat of Tribalism," *Atlantic*, Oct. 2018, 81, theatlantic.com.
14. Henry John Temple, Viscount Palmerston, remarks in the House of Commons, Mar. 1, 1848, in Bartlett, *Bartlett's Familiar Quotations*, 392; emphasis added.

SATURDAY AFTERNOON SESSION

OCTOBER 3, 2020

SUSTAINABLE SOCIETIES

ELDER D. TODD CHRISTOFFERSON

Of the Quorum of the Twelve Apostles

In 2015 the United Nations adopted what was called "The 2030 Agenda for Sustainable Development." It was described as "a shared blueprint for peace and prosperity for people and the planet, now and into the future." The Agenda for Sustainable Development includes 17 goals to be achieved by the year 2030, such as no poverty, zero hunger, quality education, gender equality, clean water and sanitation, and decent work.[1]

The concept of sustainable development is an interesting and important one. Even more urgent, however, is the broader question of sustainable societies. What are the fundamentals that sustain a flourishing society, one that promotes happiness, progress, peace, and well-being among its members? We have scriptural record of at least two such thriving societies. What can we learn from them?

Anciently, the great patriarch and prophet Enoch preached righteousness and "built a city that was called the City of Holiness, even Zion."[2] It is reported that "the Lord called his people Zion, because they were of one heart and one mind, and dwelt in righteousness; and there was no poor among them."[3]

"And the Lord blessed the land, and they were blessed upon the mountains, and upon the high places, and did flourish."[4]

The first- and second-century peoples in the Western Hemisphere known as Nephites and Lamanites provide another outstanding example of a flourishing society. Following the resurrected Savior's remarkable ministry among them, "they did walk after the commandments which they had received from their Lord and their God, continuing in fasting and prayer, and in meeting together oft both to pray and to hear the word of the Lord. . . .

"And there were no envyings, nor strifes, nor tumults, nor whoredoms, nor lyings, nor murders, nor any manner of lasciviousness; and surely there could not be a happier people among all the people who had been created by the hand of God."[5]

The societies in these two examples were sustained by the blessings of heaven growing out of their exemplary devotion to the two great commandments: "Thou shalt love the Lord thy God with all thy heart, and with all thy soul, and with all thy mind" and "Thou shalt love thy neighbour as thyself."[6] They were obedient to God in their personal lives, and they looked after one another's physical and spiritual welfare. In the words of the Doctrine and Covenants, these were societies with "every man seeking the interest of his neighbor, and doing all things with an eye single to the glory of God."[7]

Unfortunately, as Elder Quentin L. Cook noted this morning, the ideal society described in 4 Nephi of the Book of Mormon did not endure beyond its second century. Sustainability is not guaranteed, and a thriving society can fail in time if it abandons the cardinal virtues that uphold its peace and prosperity. In this case, yielding to the temptations of the devil, the people "began to be divided into classes; and they began to build up churches unto themselves to get gain, and began to deny the true church of Christ."[8]

"And it came to pass that when three hundred years had passed away, both the people of Nephi and the Lamanites had become exceedingly wicked one like unto another."[9]

By the end of another century, millions had died in internecine warfare, and their once harmonious nation had been reduced to warring tribes.

Reflecting on this and other examples of once flourishing societies that later foundered, I think it safe to say that when people turn from a sense of accountability to God and begin to trust instead in the "arm of flesh," disaster lurks. Trusting in the arm of flesh is to ignore the divine Author of human rights and human dignity and to give highest priority to riches, power, and the praise of the world (while often mocking and persecuting those who follow a different standard). Meanwhile, those in sustainable societies are seeking, as King Benjamin said, to "grow in the knowledge of the glory of him that created [them], or in the knowledge of that which is just and true."[10]

The institutions of family and religion have been crucial for endowing both individuals and communities with the virtues that sustain an enduring society. These virtues, rooted in scripture, include integrity, responsibility and accountability, compassion, marriage and fidelity in marriage, respect for others and the property of others, service, and the necessity and dignity of work, among others.

Editor-at-large Gerard Baker wrote a column earlier this year in the *Wall Street Journal* honoring his father, Frederick Baker, on the occasion of his father's 100th birthday. Baker speculated about the reasons for his father's longevity but then added these thoughts:

"While we may all want to know the secret to a long life, I often feel we'd be better off devoting more time to figuring out what makes a good life, whatever span we're allotted. Here, I'm confident I know my father's secret.

"He is from an era when life was defined primarily by duty, not by entitlement; by social responsibilities, not personal privileges. The primary animating principle throughout his century has been a sense of obligation—to family, God, country.

"In an era dominated by the detritus of broken families, my father was a devoted husband to his wife of 46 years, a dutiful father to six children. He was never more present and vital than when my parents suffered the unthinkable tragedy of losing a child. . . .

"And in an era when religion is increasingly a curiosity, my father has lived as a true, faithful Catholic, with an unshakable belief in the promises of Christ. Indeed, I sometimes think he has lived so long because he is better prepared than anyone I have ever met to die.

"I have been a fortunate man—blessed by a good education, my own wonderful family, some worldly success I didn't deserve. But however proud and grateful I feel, it's eclipsed by the pride and gratitude I have for the man who, without fuss or drama, without expectation of reward or even acknowledgment, has got on—for a century now—with the simple duties, obligations and, ultimately, joys of living a virtuous life."[11]

The perceived importance of religion and religious faith has declined in many nations in recent years. A growing number of people consider that belief in and allegiance to God are not needed for moral uprightness in either individuals or societies in today's world.[12] I think we would all agree that those who profess no religious belief can be, and often are, good, moral people. We would not agree, however, that this happens without divine influence. I am referring to the Light of Christ. The Savior declared, "I am the true light that lighteth every man that cometh into the world."[13] Whether aware of it or not, every man, woman, and child of every belief, place, and time is imbued with the Light of Christ and therefore possesses the sense of right and wrong we often call conscience.[14]

Nevertheless, when secularization separates personal and civic virtue from a sense of accountability to God, it cuts the plant from its roots. Reliance on culture and tradition alone will not be sufficient to sustain virtue in society. When one has no higher god than himself and seeks no greater good than satisfying his own appetites and preferences, the effects will be manifest in due course.

A society, for example, in which individual consent is the only constraint on sexual activity is a society in decay. Adultery, promiscuity, out-of-wedlock births,[15] and elective abortions are but some of the bitter fruits that grow out of the ongoing sexual revolution. Follow-on consequences that work against sustainability of a healthy society include growing numbers of children raised in poverty and without the positive influence of fathers, sometimes through multiple generations; women bearing alone what should be shared responsibilities; and seriously deficient education as schools, like other institutions, are tasked to compensate for failure in the home. Added to these social pathologies are the incalculable instances of individual heartbreak and despair—mental and emotional destruction visited upon both the guilty and the innocent.

Nephi proclaims:

"Wo be unto him that hearkeneth unto the precepts of men, and denieth the power of God, and the gift of the Holy Ghost! . . .

". . . Wo unto all those who tremble, and are angry because of the truth of God!"[16]

In contrast, our joyous message to our children and to all

humanity is that "the truth of God" points a better way, or as Paul said, "a more excellent way,"[17] a way to personal happiness and community well-being now and to everlasting peace and joy hereafter.

The truth of God refers to the core truths that underlie His plan of happiness for His children. These truths are that God lives; that He is the Heavenly Father of our spirits; that as a manifestation of His love, He has given us commandments that lead to a fulness of joy with Him; that Jesus Christ is the Son of God and our Redeemer; that He suffered and died to atone for sins on condition of our repentance; that He rose from the dead, bringing to pass the Resurrection of all humankind; and that we will all stand before Him to be judged, that is, to account for our lives.[18]

Nine years into what was called "the reign of the judges" in the Book of Mormon, the prophet Alma resigned his position as chief judge to give full time to his leadership of the Church. His purpose was to address the pride, persecution, and greed that were growing among the people and particularly among members of the Church.[19] As Elder Stephen D. Nadauld once observed, "[Alma's] inspired decision was not to spend more time trying to make and enforce more rules to correct the behavior of his people, but to speak to them of the word of God, to teach the doctrine and have their understanding of the plan of redemption lead them to change their behavior."[20]

There is much we can do as neighbors and fellow citizens to contribute to the sustainability and success of the societies we live in, and surely our most fundamental and enduring service will be to teach and live by the truths inherent in God's great plan of redemption. As expressed in the words of the hymn:

Faith of our fathers, we will love
Both friend and foe in all our strife,
And preach thee, too, as love knows how,
By kindly words and virtuous life.[21]

If enough of us and enough of our neighbors strive to make our decisions and guide our lives by the truth of God, the moral virtues needed in every society will abound.

In His love, our Heavenly Father gave His Only Begotten Son, Jesus Christ, that we might have everlasting life.[22]

"[Jesus Christ] doeth not anything save it be for the benefit of the world; for he loveth the world, even that he layeth down his own life that he may draw all men unto him. Wherefore, he commandeth none that they shall not partake of his salvation.

"Behold, doth he cry unto any, saying: Depart from me? Behold, I say unto you, Nay; but he saith: Come unto me all ye ends of the earth, buy milk and honey, without money and without price."[23]

This we declare "in solemnity of heart, in the spirit of meekness,"[24] and in the name of Jesus Christ, amen.

Notes

1. See "The 17 Goals," United Nations Department of Economic and Social Affairs website, sdgs.un.org/goals.
2. Moses 7:19.
3. Moses 7:18.
4. Moses 7:17.
5. 4 Nephi 1:12, 16.
6. Matthew 22:37, 39.
7. Doctrine and Covenants 82:19.
8. 4 Nephi 1:26.
9. 4 Nephi 1:45.
10. Mosiah 4:12.
11. Gerard Baker, "A Man for All Seasons at 100," *Wall Street Journal*, Feb. 21, 2020, wsj.com.
12. See Ronald F. Inglehart, "Giving Up on God: The Global Decline of Religion," *Foreign Affairs*, Sept./Oct. 2020, foreignaffairs.com; see also Christine Tamir, Aidan Connaughton, and Ariana Monique Salazar, "The Global God Divide," Pew Research Center, July 20, 2020, especially infographic "Majorities in Emerging Economies Connect Belief in God and Morality," pewresearch.org.
13. Doctrine and Covenants 93:2; see also Moroni 7:16, 19.
14. See Boyd K. Packer, "The Light of Christ," *Ensign* or *Liahona*, Apr. 2005, 10; see also D. Todd Christofferson, "Truth Endures," *Religious Educator*, vol. 19, no. 3 (2018), 6.
15. In giving this example, I am speaking of potential adverse consequences to children as "bitter fruit" and not of the children themselves. Every child of God is precious, and every life has priceless value regardless of the circumstances of birth.
16. 2 Nephi 28:26, 28.
17. 1 Corinthians 12:31.
18. See Alma 33:22.
19. See Alma 4:6–19.
20. Stephen D. Nadauld, *Principles of Priesthood Leadership* (1999), 13; see also Alma 31:5.
21. "Faith of Our Fathers," *Hymns*, no. 84.
22. See John 3:16.
23. 2 Nephi 26:24–25; see also 2 Nephi 26:33.
24. Doctrine and Covenants 100:7.

FINDING JOY IN CHRIST

STEVEN J. LUND
Young Men General President

The Lord does not ask our Aaronic Priesthood youth to do everything, but what He does ask is awe-inspiring.

A few years ago, our little family went through what many families face in this fallen world. Our youngest son, Tanner Christian Lund, contracted cancer. He was an incredible soul, as nine-year-olds tend to be. He was hilariously mischievous and, at the same time, stunningly spiritually aware. Imp and angel, naughty and nice. When he was little and was every day bewildering us with his shenanigans, we wondered if he was going to grow up to be the prophet or a bank robber. Either way, it seemed that he was going to leave a mark on the world.

And then he became desperately ill. Over the next three years, modern medicine employed heroic measures, including two bone marrow transplants, where he caught pneumonia, requiring him to spend 10 weeks unconscious on a ventilator. Miraculously, he recovered for a short time, but then his cancer returned.

Shortly before he passed away, Tanner's disease had invaded his bones, and even with strong pain medicines, still he hurt. He could barely get out of bed. One Sunday morning, his mom, Kalleen, came into his room to check on him before the family left for church. She was surprised to see that he had somehow gotten himself dressed and was sitting on the edge of his bed, painfully struggling to button his shirt. Kalleen sat down by him. "Tanner," she said, "are you sure you are strong enough to go to church? Maybe you should stay home and rest today."

He stared at the floor. He was a deacon. He had a quorum. And he had an assignment.

"I'm supposed to pass the sacrament today."

"Well, I'm sure someone could do that for you."

"Yes," he said, "but . . . I see how people look at me when I pass the sacrament. I think it helps them."

So Kalleen helped him button his shirt and tie his tie, and they drove to church. Clearly, something important was happening.

I came to church from an earlier meeting and so was surprised to see Tanner sitting on the deacons' row. Kalleen quietly told me why he was there and what he had said: "It helps people."

And so I watched as the deacons stepped to the sacrament table. He leaned gently against another deacon as the priests passed them the bread trays. And then Tanner shuffled to his appointed place and took hold of the end of the pew to steady himself as he presented the sacrament.

It seemed that every eye in the chapel was on him, moved by his struggle as he did his simple part. Somehow Tanner expressed a silent sermon as he solemnly, haltingly moved from row to row—his bald head moist with perspiration—representing the Savior in the way that deacons do. His once indomitable deacon's body was itself a little bruised, broken, and torn, willingly suffering to serve by bearing the emblems of the Savior's Atonement into our lives.

Seeing how he had come to think about being a deacon made us think differently too—about the sacrament, about the Savior, and about deacons and teachers and priests.

I wonder at the unspoken miracle that had impelled him that morning to respond so bravely to that still, small call to serve, and about the strength and capacities of all of our emergent youth as they push themselves to respond to a prophet's call to enlist in God's battalions and join in the work of salvation and exaltation.

Every time a deacon holds a sacrament tray, we are reminded of the sacred story of the Last Supper, of Gethsemane, of Calvary, and of the garden tomb. When the Savior said to His Apostles, "This do in remembrance of me,"[1] He was also speaking through the ages to each of us. He was speaking of the unending miracle that He would provide as future deacons, teachers, and priests would present His emblems and invite His children to accept His atoning gift.

All of the sacramental symbols point us to that gift. We contemplate the bread that He once broke—and the bread the priests before us are, in turn, now breaking. We think of the meaning of the liquid consecrated, then and now, as sacrament prayers solemnly pass from the mouths of young priests into our hearts and into the heavens, renewing covenants that connect us to the very powers of Christ's salvation. We may think about what it means when a deacon carries the sacred emblems to us, standing as he does where Jesus would stand if He were there, offering to lift our burdens and our pain.

Fortunately, young men and women do not have to get sick to discover joy and purpose in serving the Savior.

Elder David A. Bednar has taught that to grow and become as missionaries *are,* we should do what missionaries *do,* and then, "line upon line and precept upon precept, . . . [we] can gradually become the missionary . . . the Savior expects."[2]

Likewise, if we desire "to be like Jesus,"[3] we should do what Jesus does, and in one astonishing sentence, the Lord explains what it is that He does: He said, "For behold, this is my work and my glory—to bring to pass the immortality and eternal life of man."[4]

The Savior's mission has always and forever been to serve His Father by saving His children.

And the surest way to find joy in this life is to join Christ in helping others.

This is the simple truth that inspired the Children and Youth program.

All Children and Youth activities and all Children and Youth teachings are about helping young people become more like Jesus by joining with Him in His work of salvation and exaltation.

Children and Youth is a tool to help every Primary child and youth to grow in discipleship and to gain a faith-filled vision of what the way of happiness looks like. They can come to anticipate and yearn for the way stations and signposts along the covenant path, where they will be baptized and confirmed with the gift of the Holy Ghost and soon belong to quorums and Young Women classes, where they will feel the joy of helping others through a succession of Christlike acts of service. They will set goals, large and small, that will bring balance to their lives as they become more like the Savior.

For the Strength of Youth conferences and magazines, the *Friend,* and the Gospel Living app will help center them in finding joy in Christ. They will anticipate the blessings of holding limited-use temple recommends and feel the spirit of Elijah through the influence of the Holy Ghost as they pursue the blessings of the temple and family history. They will be guided by patriarchal blessings. In time, they will see themselves going into temples to be endowed with power and to find joy there as they are eternally connected, come what may, with their families.

Against headwinds of pandemic and calamity, bringing about the full promise of the new Children and Youth program is still a work in progress—but there is urgency. Our youth cannot wait for the world to right itself before they come to know the Savior. Some are making decisions even now that they would not make if they understood their true identities—and His.

And so the urgent call from God's battalions in fateful training is for "all hands on deck!"

Moms and dads, your sons need you to support them now as passionately as ever you have in the past when they have been about lesser things like badges and pins. Mothers and fathers, priesthood and Young Women leaders, if your youth are struggling, Children and Youth will help bring them to the Savior, and the Savior will bring them peace.

Quorum and class presidencies, step up and take your rightful place in the Lord's work.

Bishops, link your keys with those of quorum presidents, and your quorums—and your wards—will forever change.

And to you of the rising generation, I testify, as one who knows, that you *are* beloved sons and daughters of God and He has a work for you to do.

As you rise to the majesty of your stations, with all of your hearts, might, mind, and strength, you will come to love God and keep your covenants and trust in His priesthood as you work to bless others, beginning in your own homes.

I pray that you will strive, with redoubled energy worthy of this time, to serve, exercise faith, repent, and improve each day, to qualify to receive temple blessings and the enduring joy that comes only through the gospel of Jesus Christ. I pray that you will prepare to become that diligent missionary, loyal husband or wife, loving father or mother that you have been promised you may ultimately become by being a true disciple of Jesus Christ.

May you help prepare the world for the Savior's return by inviting all to come unto Christ and receive the blessings of His Atonement. In the name of Jesus Christ, amen.

Notes

1. Luke 22:19.
2. David A. Bednar, "Becoming a Missionary," *Ensign* or *Liahona*, Nov. 2005, 46.
3. "I'm trying to be like Jesus; I'm following in his ways. I'm trying to love as he did, in all that I do and say" ("I'm Trying to Be like Jesus," *Children's Songbook*, 78–79).
4. Moses 1:39.

ALL NATIONS, KINDREDS, AND TONGUES

ELDER GERRIT W. GONG
Of the Quorum of the Twelve Apostles

Dear brothers and sisters, I recently officiated in a temple sealing, following COVID-19 guidelines. With the bride and groom, both faithful returned missionaries, were their parents and all their siblings. This was not easy. The bride is the ninth of ten children. Her nine siblings sat in order, oldest to youngest, socially distanced of course.

The family had sought to be good neighbors wherever they lived. However, one community had been unwelcoming—because, the bride's mother said, their family were members of The Church of Jesus Christ of Latter-day Saints.

The family did everything to make friends at school, contribute, and be accepted, but to no avail. The family prayed and prayed hearts would soften.

One night, the family felt their prayers were answered, though in a very unexpected way. Their house caught fire and burned to the ground. But something else happened. The fire softened their neighbors' hearts.

Their neighbors and local school gathered clothes, shoes, and other necessities needed by the family, who had lost everything. Kindness opened understanding. It was not the way the family hoped or expected their prayers to be answered. However, they express gratitude for what they learned through hard experiences and unexpected answers to heartfelt prayers.

Truly, for those with faithful hearts and eyes to see, the Lord's tender mercies are manifest amidst life's challenges. Faithfully met challenges and sacrifice do bring the blessings of heaven. In this mortality, we may lose or wait for some things for a time, but in the end we will find what matters most.[1] That is His promise.[2]

Our 2020 bicentennial proclamation begins with the profoundly inclusive promise that "God loves His children in every nation of the world."[3] To each of us in every nation, kindred, tongue, and people,[4] God promises, covenants, and invites us to come partake of His abundant joy and goodness.

God's love for all people is affirmed throughout scripture.[5] That love encompasses the Abrahamic covenant, gathering His scattered children,[6] and His plan of happiness in our lives.

In the household of faith there are to be no strangers, no foreigners,[7] no rich and poor,[8] no outside "others." As "fellowcitizens with the saints,"[9] we are invited to change the world for the better, from the inside out, one person, one family, one neighborhood at a time.

This happens when we live and share the gospel. Early in this dispensation, the Prophet Joseph received a remarkable prophecy that Heavenly Father desires everyone everywhere to discover God's love and experience His power to grow and change.

That prophecy was received here, at the Smith family log home in Palmyra, New York.[10]

Completed in 1998, the Smith home is reconstructed on its original foundation. The second-story bedroom occupies the same 18- by 30- by 10-foot (5.5 by 9 by 3m) physical space where Moroni, as a glorious messenger from God, came to the young Joseph on the evening of September 21, 1823.[11]

You remember what the Prophet Joseph recounted:

"[Moroni] said . . . God had a work for me to do; and that my name should be had for good and evil among all nations, kindreds, and tongues. . . .

"[Moroni] said there was a book deposited, . . . that the fulness of the everlasting Gospel was contained in it."[12]

Here we pause. We worship God the Eternal Father and His Son, Jesus Christ, not the Prophet Joseph nor any mortal man or woman.

Yet consider how the prophecies God gives His servants are fulfilled.[13] Some are fulfilled earlier, some later, but all are fulfilled.[14] As we hearken to the Lord's spirit of prophecy, we can become, in our own way, part of the fulfillment of His prophecies and promises—part of the gospel blessing the world.

In 1823, Joseph was an unknown 17-year-old boy living in an obscure village in a newly independent country. Unless it were true, how would he imagine to say he would be an instrument in God's work and translate by God's gift and power sacred scripture that would become known everywhere?

Yet, because it is true, you and I can witness that prophecy being fulfilled even as we are invited to help bring it to pass.

Brothers and sisters, across the world, each of us participating in this October 2020 general conference is among the nations, kindreds, and tongues spoken of.

Today, members of The Church of Jesus Christ of Latter-day Saints live in 196 nations and territories, with 3,446 Church stakes in 90 of them.[15] We represent both geographic breadth and centers of strength.

In 1823, who would have imagined that in the year 2020 there would be three countries each with more than a million members of this Church—the United States, Mexico, and Brazil?

Or 23 countries each with more than 100,000 members of the Church—three in North America, fourteen in Central and South America, one in Europe, four in Asia, and one in Africa?[16]

President Russell M. Nelson calls the Book of Mormon "a miraculous miracle."[17] Its witnesses testify, "Be it known unto all nations, kindreds, tongues, and people."[18] Today, general conference is available in 100 languages. President Nelson has testified of Jesus Christ and His restored gospel in 138 nations and counting.

Beginning with 5,000 printed copies of the 1830 first edition of the Book of Mormon, some 192 million copies of all or part of the Book of Mormon have been published in 112 languages. Book of Mormon translations are also widely available digitally. Current Book of Mormon translations include most of the 23 world languages spoken by 50 million people or more, collectively the native tongues of some 4.1 billion people.[19]

By small and simple means—in which we are each invited to participate—great things are brought to pass.

For example, at a stake conference in Monroe, Utah, population 2,200, I asked how many had served missions. Nearly every hand went up. In recent years, from that one stake, 564 missionaries have served in all 50 U.S. states and 53 countries—on every continent except Antarctica.

Speaking of Antarctica, even in Ushuaia, at the southern tip of Argentina, I saw prophecy being fulfilled as our missionaries shared the restored gospel of Jesus Christ in a place called "the end of the earth."[20]

The mural formed by the covers of our four volumes of *Saints*[21] depicts a global tapestry of the fruits of gospel living coming to faithful Saints everywhere. Our Church history is anchored in the lived testimony and gospel journey of each member, including Mary Whitmer, the faithful sister to whom Moroni showed the Book of Mormon plates.[22]

Coming in January 2021, our three new global Church magazines —the *Friend, For the Strength of Youth,* and the *Liahona*—invite all to belong and share experiences and testimony in our worldwide community of faith.[23]

Brothers and sisters, as we increase our faith in Heavenly Father and Jesus Christ, receive the blessings found in living restored gospel truths and sacred covenants, and study, ponder, and share about the ongoing Restoration, we participate in fulfilling prophecy.

We are changing ourselves and the world in a gospel pattern that blesses lives everywhere.

An African sister says, "My husband's priesthood service makes him more patient and kind. And I am becoming a better wife and mother."

A now-respected international business consultant in Central America says before he discovered God's restored gospel, he lived aimlessly on the street. Now he and his family have found identity, purpose, and strength.

A young boy in South America raises chickens and sells their eggs to help buy windows for the house his family is building. He pays his tithing first. He will literally see the windows of heaven open.

In Four Corners, a community in the southwestern United States, a Native American family grows a beautiful rose bush to blossom in the desert, symbolic of gospel faith and self-reliance.

A survivor of bitter civil war, a brother in Southeast Asia despaired that life had no meaning. He found hope in a dream in which a former classmate held a sacrament tray and testified of saving ordinances and the Atonement of Jesus Christ.

Heavenly Father invites us everywhere to feel His love, to learn and grow through education, honorable work, self-reliant service, and patterns of goodness and happiness we find in His restored Church.

As we come to trust God, sometimes through pleading in our darkest, loneliest, most uncertain moments, we learn He knows us better and loves us more than we know or love ourselves.

This is why we need God's help to create lasting justice, equality, fairness, and peace in our homes and communities. Our truest, deepest, most authentic narrative, place, and belonging come when we feel God's redeeming love, seek grace and miracles through His Son's Atonement, and establish lasting relationships by sacred covenants.

Religious goodness and wisdom are needed in today's cluttered, noisy, polluted world. How else can we refresh, inspire, and edify the human spirit?[24]

Planting trees in Haiti is only one among hundreds of examples of people coming together to do good. The local community, including 1,800 members of our Church, which donated the trees, gathered to plant nearly 25,000 trees.[25] This multiyear reforestation project has already planted over 121,000 trees. It anticipates planting tens of thousands more.

This united effort provides shade, conserves soil, abates future floods. It beautifies neighborhoods, builds community, satisfies taste, and nourishes the soul. If you ask Haitians who will harvest the fruit from these trees, they say, "Whoever is hungry."

Some 80 percent of the world's population are religiously affiliated.[26] Religious communities readily respond to immediate needs after natural disasters as well as to chronic needs for food, shelter, education, literacy, and employment training. Across the world, our members, friends, and Church help communities support refugees and provide water, sanitation, handicap mobility, and vision care—one person, one village, one tree at a time.[27] Everywhere, we seek to be good parents and good citizens, to contribute in our neighborhoods and societies, including through Latter-day Saint Charities.[28]

God gives us moral agency—and moral accountability. Declares the Lord, "I, the Lord God, make you free, therefore [you] are free indeed."[29] In proclaiming "liberty to the captives,"[30] the Lord promises His Atonement and gospel path can break temporal and spiritual bonds.[31] Mercifully, this redemptive freedom extends to those who have passed from mortality.

Some years ago, a priest in Central America told me he was studying Latter-day Saint "baptism for deceased persons." "It does seem just," the priest said, "that God would offer every person opportunity to receive baptism, no matter when or where they lived, except little children, who 'are alive in Christ.'[32] The Apostle Paul," the priest noted, "speaks of the dead awaiting baptism and resurrection."[33] Vicarious temple ordinances promise all nations, kindreds, and tongues that no one need "remain a slave of death, of hell, or of the grave."[34]

As we discover God, sometimes unexpected answers to prayers take us from the street, bring us to community, chase darkness from our souls, and guide us to find spiritual refuge and belonging in the goodness of His covenants and abiding love.

Great things often begin small, but God's miracles are manifest daily. How grateful we are for the supernal gift of the Holy Ghost, the Atonement of Jesus Christ, and His revealed doctrine, ordinances, and covenants found in His restored Church, called in His name.

May we joyfully accept God's invitation to receive and help fulfill His promised and prophesied blessings in all nations, kindreds, and tongues, I pray in the sacred and holy name of Jesus Christ, amen.

Notes

1. "All your losses will be made up to you in the resurrection, provided you continue faithful" (*Teachings of Presidents of the Church: Joseph Smith* [2007], 51).
2. See Mosiah 2:41.
3. "The Restoration of the Fulness of the Gospel of Jesus Christ: A Bicentennial Proclamation to the World," ChurchofJesusChrist.org; see also, for example, Alma 26:37.

4. See Revelation 14:6; 1 Nephi 19:17; 22:28; 2 Nephi 30:8; Mosiah 3:20; 15:28; Alma 37:4–6; 3 Nephi 28:29; Doctrine and Covenants 42:58; 133:37.
5. See John 3:16–17; 15:12; Romans 8:35, 38–39.
6. See 1 Nephi 22:3, 9; Doctrine and Covenants 45:24–25, 69, 71; 64:42.
7. See Ephesians 2:19.
8. See Doctrine and Covenants 104:14–17.
9. Ephesians 2:19.
10. A few hundred yards from the Smith home back door is a grove of trees, which became our Sacred Grove "the morning of a beautiful, clear day, early in the spring of eighteen hundred and twenty" (Joseph Smith—History 1:14).
11. Being in the specific, physical location of a known historical event can powerfully connect time and place. Still, our testimony of the sacred events surrounding Moroni's appearance to the young Prophet Joseph is spiritual.
12. Joseph Smith—History 1:33–34.
13. See Amos 3:7; Doctrine and Covenants 1:38.
14. See Alma 37:6; Doctrine and Covenants 64:33.
15. Church statistics as of September 3, 2020; "nations and territories" include entities such as Guam, Puerto Rico, and American Samoa.
16. The 23 countries are the United States, Mexico, Brazil, the Philippines, Peru, Chile, Argentina, Guatemala, Ecuador, Bolivia, Colombia, Canada, the United Kingdom, Honduras, Nigeria, Venezuela, Australia, Dominican Republic, Japan, El Salvador, New Zealand, Uruguay, and Nicaragua. Australia and New Zealand are included in the four countries in Asia with over 100,000 members. Paraguay has over 96,000 Church members and may be next to join the 100,000-member group.
17. Russell M. Nelson, "The Book of Mormon: A Miraculous Miracle" (address given at the seminar for new mission presidents, June 23, 2016).
18. "The Testimony of Three Witnesses" and "The Testimony of Eight Witnesses," Book of Mormon.
19. Additional translations continue the promise that every man and woman will "hear the fulness of the gospel in his [or her] own tongue, and . . . language" (Doctrine and Covenants 90:11).
20. See Doctrine and Covenants 122:1.
21. The titles of the four volumes of *Saints* come from the inspired testimony declaration of the Prophet Joseph in the Wentworth letter—*The Standard of Truth; No Unhallowed Hand; Boldly, Nobly, and Independent;* and *Sounded in Every Ear.*
22. See *Saints: The Story of the Church of Jesus Christ in the Latter Days*, vol. 1, *The Standard of Truth, 1815–1846* (2018), 70–71.
23. See First Presidency letter, Aug. 14, 2020.
24. See Gerrit W. Gong, "Seven Ways Religious Inputs and Values Contribute to Practical, Principle-Based Policy Approaches" (address given at the G20 Interfaith Forum, June 8, 2019), newsroom.ChurchofJesusChrist.org.
25. See Jason Swensen, "LDS Church Celebrates 30 Years in Haiti by Planting Thousands of Trees," *Deseret News*, May 1, 2013, deseretnews.com.
26. See Pew Research Center, "The Global Religious Landscape," Dec. 18, 2012, pewforum.org. This "comprehensive demographic study of more than 230 countries and territories . . . estimates that there are 5.8 billion religiously affiliated adults and children around the globe, representing 84% of the 2010 world population of 6.9 billion."
27. Religious virtues and values anchor and enrich civil society; inspire community, civil engagement, social cohesion, service, and volunteerism; and foster justice, reconciliation, and forgiveness, including helping us to know when and how to hold on and to let go, to know when and what to remember and to forget.
28. In addition to their contributions to Latter-day Saint Charities (see latterdaysaintcharities.org), which serves as the humanitarian arm of the Church, members of The Church of Jesus Christ of Latter-day Saints join their neighbors and communities in giving of time and means through service in JustServe or Helping Hands projects (see justserve.org and ChurchofJesusChrist.org/topics/humanitarian-service/helping-hands) and through the donation of fast offerings (see "Fasting and Fast Offerings," Gospel Topics, topics.ChurchofJesusChrist.org). Each of these

efforts takes the significant generosity of Church members and friends to bless thousands across the world.
29. Doctrine and Covenants 98:8.
30. Isaiah 61:1; see also John 8:36; Galatians 5:1; Doctrine and Covenants 88:86.
31. This hope of freedom includes those seeking to overcome debilitating habits or addictions, self-defeating behaviors, intergenerational guilt, or any sorrow.
32. Moroni 8:12; see also Doctrine and Covenants 137:10.
33. See 1 Corinthians 15:29.
34. "While of These Emblems We Partake," *Hymns*, no. 173, verse 3.

THERE WAS BREAD

BISHOP W. CHRISTOPHER WADDELL
First Counselor in the Presiding Bishopric

Prior to travel restrictions caused by the current pandemic, I was returning home from an international assignment which, due to scheduling issues, created a Sunday layover. I had time between flights to attend a local sacrament meeting, where I was also able to share a brief message. Following the meeting, an enthusiastic deacon approached me and asked if I knew President Nelson and if I had ever had a chance to shake his hand. I answered that I did know him, that I had shaken his hand, and that, as a member of the Presiding Bishopric, I had the opportunity to meet with President Nelson and his counselors a couple of times each week.

The young deacon then sat down on a chair, threw his hands in the air, and shouted, "This is the greatest day of my life!" Brothers and sisters, I may not throw my hands in the air and shout, but I am eternally grateful for a living prophet and for the direction we receive from prophets, seers, and revelators, especially during these times of challenge.

From the beginning of time, the Lord has provided direction to help His people prepare spiritually and temporally against the calamities and trials that He knows will come as part of this mortal experience. These calamities may be personal or general in nature, but the Lord's guidance will provide protection and support to the extent that we heed and act upon His counsel. A wonderful example is provided in an account from the book of Genesis, where we learn of Joseph in Egypt and his inspired interpretation of Pharaoh's dream.

"And Joseph said unto Pharaoh, . . . God hath shewed Pharaoh what he is about to do. . . .

"Behold, there come seven years of great plenty throughout all the land of Egypt:

"And there shall arise after them seven years of famine; and all the plenty shall be forgotten in the land of Egypt."[1]

Pharaoh listened to Joseph, responded to what God had showed him in a dream, and immediately set about preparing for what was to come. The scriptures then record:

"And in the seven plenteous years the earth brought forth by handfuls.

"And he gathered up all the food of the seven years. . . .

"And Joseph gathered corn as the sand of the sea, . . . until he left numbering; for it was without number."[2]

Once the seven years of plenty had passed, we are told that "seven years of dearth began to come, according as Joseph had said: and the dearth was in all lands; but in all the land of Egypt there was bread."[3]

Today we are blessed to be led by prophets who understand the need for us to prepare against the calamities "which should come"[4] and who also recognize the limitations or restrictions that we may encounter in striving to follow their counsel.

There is a clear understanding that the effects of COVID-19, as well as devastating natural disasters, are no respecter of persons and cross ethnic, social, and religious boundaries on every continent. Jobs have been lost and incomes reduced as the opportunity to work has been affected by layoffs and the ability to work has been impacted by health and legal challenges.

To all who have been affected, we express understanding and concern for your situation, as well as a firm conviction that better days are ahead. You have been blessed with bishops and branch presidents who seek out members of their congregations with temporal needs and who have access to tools and resources that can help you reestablish your lives and place you on the path to self-reliance as you apply principles of preparedness.

In today's environment, with a pandemic that has devastated whole economies as well as individual lives, it would be inconsistent with a compassionate Savior to ignore the reality that many are struggling and ask them to begin building a reserve of food and money for the future. However, that does not mean that we should permanently ignore principles of preparation—only that these principles should be applied "in wisdom and order"[5] so that in the future we might say, as did Joseph in Egypt, "There was bread."[6]

The Lord does not expect us to do more than we can do, but He does expect us to do what we can do, when we can do it. As President Nelson reminded us in our last general conference, "The Lord loves effort."[7]

Church leaders have often encouraged Latter-day Saints "to prepare for adversity in life by having a basic supply of food and water and some money in savings."[8] At the same time, we are encouraged to "be wise" and "not go to extremes"[9] in our efforts to establish a home storage supply and a financial reserve. A resource entitled *Personal Finances for Self-Reliance,* published in 2017 and currently available on the Church website in 36 languages, begins with a message from the First Presidency, which states:

"The Lord has declared, 'It is my purpose to provide for my saints' [Doctrine and Covenants 104:15]. This revelation is a promise from the Lord that He will provide temporal blessings and open the door of self-reliance. . . .

". . . Accepting and living these principles will better enable you to receive the temporal blessings promised by the Lord.

"We invite you to diligently study and apply these principles and teach them to your family members. As you do so, your life will be blessed . . . [because] you are a child of our Father in Heaven. He loves you and will never forsake you. He knows you and is ready to extend to you the spiritual and temporal blessings of self-reliance."[10]

This resource includes chapters devoted to creating and living within a budget, protecting your family against hardship, managing a financial crisis, investing for the future, and many more and is available for everyone on the Church website or through your local leaders.

When considering the principle of preparedness, we can look back to Joseph in Egypt for inspiration. Knowing what would happen would not have been sufficient to carry them through the "lean" years without a degree of sacrifice during the years of abundance. Rather than consume all that Pharaoh's subjects could produce, limits were established and followed, providing sufficient for their immediate, as well as their future, needs. It was not enough to know that challenging times would come. They had to act, and because of their effort, "there was bread."[11]

This leads to an important question: "Therefore, what?" A good place to begin is to understand that all things are spiritual to the Lord, "and not at any time" has He given us "a law which was temporal."[12] Everything, then, points to Jesus Christ as the foundation upon which we must build even our temporal preparedness.

Being temporally prepared and self-reliant means "believing that through the grace, or enabling power, of Jesus Christ and our own effort, we are able to obtain all the spiritual and temporal necessities of life we require for ourselves and our families."[13]

Additional aspects of a spiritual foundation for temporal preparedness include acting "in wisdom and order,"[14] which implies a gradual buildup of food storage and savings over time, as well as embracing "small and simple" means,[15] which is a demonstration of faith that the Lord will magnify our small but consistent efforts.

With a spiritual foundation in place, we can then successfully apply two important elements of temporal preparedness—managing finances and home storage.

Key principles to manage your finances include the payment of tithes and offerings, eliminating and avoiding debt, preparing and living within a budget, and saving for the future.

Key home storage principles include the storage of food, the storage of water, and the storage of other necessities based on individual and family needs, all because "the best storehouse"[16] is the home, which becomes the "most accessible reserve in times of need."[17]

As we embrace spiritual principles and seek inspiration from the Lord, we will be guided to know the Lord's will for us, individually and as families, and how best to apply the important principles of temporal preparedness. The most important step of all is to begin.

Elder David A. Bednar taught this principle when he said: "Taking action is the exercise of faith. . . . True faith is focused in and on the Lord Jesus Christ and always leads to action."[18]

Brothers and sisters, in an ever-changing world, we must prepare for uncertainties. Even with better days ahead, we know that the temporal peaks and valleys of mortality will continue. As we seek to become temporally prepared, we can face the trials of life with increased confidence, peace in our hearts, and like Joseph in Egypt, we will be able to say, even in stressful circumstances, "There was bread."[19] In the name of Jesus Christ, amen.

Notes

1. See Genesis 41:25–30.
2. Genesis 41:47–49.
3. Genesis 41:54.
4. Doctrine and Covenants 1:17.
5. Mosiah 4:27.
6. Genesis 41:54.
7. Russell M. Nelson, in Joy D. Jones, "An Especially Noble Calling," *Ensign* or *Liahona*, May 2020, 16.
8. *All Is Safely Gathered In: Family Home Storage* (pamphlet, 2007), 1.
9. *All Is Safely Gathered In*, 1.
10. "Message from the First Presidency," *Personal Finances for Self-Reliance* (2017), inside front cover.
11. Genesis 41:54.
12. See Doctrine and Covenants 29:34–35.
13. *Personal Finances for Self-Reliance*, 4.
14. Mosiah 4:27.
15. Alma 37:6.
16. Gordon B. Hinckley, "If Ye Are Prepared Ye Shall Not Fear," *Ensign* or *Liahona*, Nov. 2005, 62.
17. "Emergency Preparedness," Gospel Topics, topics.ChurchofJesusChrist.org.
18. David A. Bednar, "Exercise Faith in Christ" (video), ChurchofJesusChrist.org/media.
19. Genesis 41:54.

THE EXQUISITE GIFT OF THE SON

ELDER MATTHEW S. HOLLAND
Of the Seventy

While reading the Book of Mormon for a *Come, Follow Me* lesson last summer, I was struck by Alma's report that when he became fully conscious of his sins, there was "nothing so *exquisite* and so *bitter* as were [his] pains."[1] I confess, talk of exquisite pain caught my attention partly due to my battle that week with a seven-millimeter kidney stone. Never has one man experienced such "great things" when such a "small and simple" thing was "brought to pass."[2]

Alma's language also stood out to me because the word *exquisite,* in the English translation of the Book of Mormon, typically describes things of exceptional beauty or unparalleled magnificence. For example, Joseph Smith noted that the angel Moroni wore robes of "exquisite whiteness," "a whiteness beyond anything earthly [he] had ever seen."[3] Yet *exquisite* can also convey an extreme intensity even for awful things. Thus Alma and top dictionaries link *exquisite pain* to being "tormented," "racked," and "harrowed" to the "greatest degree."[4]

Alma's imagery reflects the sobering reality that at some point the full, excruciating guilt of every sin we commit must be felt. Justice demands it, and God Himself cannot change it.[5] When Alma remembered "all" his sins—especially those that had destroyed the faith of others—his pain was virtually unbearable, and the idea of standing before God filled him with "inexpressible horror." He yearned to "become extinct both soul and body."[6]

However, Alma said everything started to change the moment his "mind caught hold upon" the prophesied "coming of one Jesus Christ . . . to atone for the sins of the world" and he "cried within [his] heart: O Jesus, thou Son of God, have mercy on me." With that one thought and that one plea, Alma was filled with "exquisite" joy "as exceeding as was [his] pain."[7]

We must never forget that the very purpose of repentance is to take certain misery and transform it into pure bliss. Thanks to His "immediate goodness,"[8] the *instant* we come unto Christ—demonstrating faith in Him and a true change of heart—the crushing weight of our sins starts to shift from our backs to His. This is possible only because He who is without sin suffered "the infinite and unspeakable agony"[9] of every single sin in the universe of His creations, for all of His creations—a suffering so severe, blood oozed out of His every pore. From direct, personal experience the Savior thus warns us, in modern scripture, that we have no idea how "exquisite" our "sufferings" will be if we do not repent. But with unfathomable generosity He also clarifies that "I, God, have suffered these things for all, that they might not suffer if they would repent"[10]—a repentance which allows us to "taste" the "exceeding joy" Alma tasted.[11] For this doctrine alone, "I stand all amazed."[12] Yet, astonishingly, Christ offers even more.

Sometimes exquisite pain comes not from sin but from honest mistakes, the actions of others, or forces beyond our control. In these moments, you may cry like the righteous Psalmist:

"My heart is sore pained within me: and the terrors of death are fallen upon me.

". . . And horror hath overwhelmed me.

". . . Oh that I had wings like a dove! for then would I fly away, and be at rest."[13]

Medical science, professional counseling, or legal rectification can help alleviate such suffering. But note, all good gifts—including these—come from the Savior.[14] Regardless of the causes of our worst hurts and heartaches, the ultimate source of relief is the same: Jesus Christ. He alone holds the full power and healing balm to correct every mistake, right every wrong, adjust every imperfection, mend every wound, and deliver every delayed blessing. Like witnesses of old, I testify that "we have not an high priest which cannot be touched with the feeling of our infirmities"[15] but rather a loving Redeemer who descended from His throne above and went forth "suffering pains and afflictions and temptations of every kind . . . , that he may know . . . how to succor his people."[16]

For anyone today with pains so intense or so unique that you feel no one else could fully appreciate them, you may have a point. There may be no family member, friend, or priesthood leader—however sensitive and well-meaning each may be—who knows exactly what you are feeling or has the precise words to help you heal. But know this: there is One who understands perfectly what you are experiencing, who is "mightier than all the earth,"[17] and who is "able to do exceeding abundantly above all that [you] ask or think."[18] The process will unfold in His way and on His schedule, but Christ stands ready *always* to heal every ounce and aspect of your agony.

As you allow Him to do so, you will discover that your suffering was not in vain. Speaking of many of the Bible's greatest heroes and their griefs, the Apostle Paul said that "God . . . provided some better things for them through their sufferings, for without sufferings they could not be made perfect."[19] You see, the very nature of God and aim of our earthly existence is happiness,[20] but we cannot become perfect beings of divine joy without experiences that test us, sometimes to our very core. Paul says even the Savior Himself was made eternally "perfect [or complete] through sufferings."[21] So guard against the satanic whispering that if you were a better person, you would avoid such trials.

You must also resist the related lie that your sufferings somehow suggest you stand outside the circle of God's chosen ones, who seem to glide from one blessed state to another. Instead, see yourself as John the Revelator surely saw you in his majestic revelation of the latter days. For John saw "a great multitude, which no man could number, of all nations, and kindreds, and people, and tongues, [who] stood before the throne, and before the Lamb, clothed with white robes, . . . [who] cried with a loud voice, saying, Salvation to our God."[22]

When asked: "What are these which are arrayed in white robes? and whence came they?" John received the answer: "These are they which came out of *great tribulation,* and have washed their robes, and made them white in the blood of the Lamb."[23]

Brothers and sisters, suffering in righteousness helps qualify you for, rather than distinguishes you from, God's elect. And it makes their promises your promises. As John declares, you "shall hunger no more, neither thirst any more; neither shall the sun light on [you], nor any heat. For the Lamb which is in the midst of the throne shall feed [you], and shall lead [you] unto living fountains of waters: and God shall wipe away all tears from [your] eyes."[24]

"And there shall be no more death, neither sorrow, nor crying, neither shall there be any more pain."[25]

I witness to you that through the staggering goodness of Jesus Christ and His infinite Atonement, we can escape the deserved agonies of our moral failings and overcome the undeserved agonies of our mortal misfortunes. Under His direction, your divine destiny will be one of unparalleled magnificence and indescribable joy—a joy so intense and so unique to you, your particular "ashes" will become beauties "beyond anything earthly."[26] That you might taste this happiness now and be filled with it forever, I invite you to do what Alma did: let your mind catch hold on the *exquisite* gift of the Son of God as revealed through His gospel in this, His true and living Church. In the name of Jesus Christ, amen.

Notes

1. Alma 36:21; emphasis added.
2. Alma 37:6.
3. Joseph Smith—History 1:31.
4. For instance, compare the explicitly similar language of Alma 36:11–17 with the entry for *exquisite* in the *Oxford American Writer's Thesaurus*—one of several publications that can be loaded in the "Dictionary" section of the general settings on certain devices and thus linked for easy access in the Gospel Library app. Thanks to Rachel Sanford for this reminder.
5. See Alma 42:13.
6. See Alma 36:13–15.
7. See Alma 36:17–21.
8. Mosiah 25:10.
9. See Orson F. Whitney, *Baptism—the Birth of Water and of Spirit* (1934), 5.
10. Doctrine and Covenants 19:15–16.
11. See Alma 36:24–26.
12. "I Stand All Amazed," *Hymns*, no. 193.
13. Psalm 55:4–6.
14. See Moroni 7:24.
15. Hebrews 4:15.
16. Alma 7:11–12.
17. 1 Nephi 4:1.
18. Ephesians 3:20.
19. Joseph Smith Translation, Hebrews 11:40 (in Hebrews 11:40, footnote a).
20. See 2 Nephi 2:25; Alma 41:11.
21. Hebrews 2:10; see also Hebrews 5:8; Russell M. Nelson, "Perfection Pending," *Ensign*, Nov. 1995, 86–88.
22. Revelation 7:9–10.
23. Revelation 7:13–14; emphasis added.
24. Revelation 7:16–17.
25. Revelation 21:4.
26. See Isaiah 61:3; Joseph Smith—History 1:31.

THE CULTURE OF CHRIST

ELDER WILLIAM K. JACKSON
Of the Seventy

What a magnificent world we live in and share, home to a great diversity of peoples, languages, customs, and histories—spread out over hundreds of countries and thousands of groups, each rich in culture. Mankind has much to be proud of and to celebrate. But though learned behavior—those things to which we are exposed by the cultures we grow up in—can serve as a great strength in our lives, it can also, at times, become a significant obstacle.

It may seem that culture is so heavily embedded in our thinking and behavior that it is impossible to change. It is, after all, much of what we feel defines us and from which we feel a sense of identity. It can be such a strong influence that we can fail to see the man-made weaknesses or flaws in our own cultures, resulting in a reluctance to throw off some of the traditions of our fathers. An overfixation on one's cultural identity may lead to the rejection of worthwhile—even godly—ideas, attributes, and behavior.

I knew a wonderful gentleman not too many years ago who helps to illustrate this universal principle of cultural myopia. I first met him in Singapore when I was assigned to be his family's home teacher. A distinguished professor of Sanskrit and Tamil, he hailed from the south of India. His wonderful wife and two sons were members of the Church, but he had never joined nor listened much to the teachings of the gospel. He was happy with the way his wife and sons were developing and supported them fully in their undertakings and Church responsibilities.

When I offered to teach him the principles of the gospel and share our beliefs with him, he initially balked. It took me a while to figure out why: he felt that by so doing, he would become a traitor to his past, his people, and his history! To his way of thinking, he would be denying everything he was, everything his family had taught him to be, his very Indian heritage. Over the next few months, we were able to talk about these issues. I was awed (though not surprised!) by how the gospel of Jesus Christ was able to open his eyes to a different viewpoint.

In most man-made cultures, there is found both good and bad, constructive and destructive.

Many of our world's problems are a direct result of clashes between those of differing ideas and customs arising from their culture. But virtually *all* conflict and chaos would quickly fade if the world would only accept its original culture, the one we all possessed not so very long ago. This culture dates back to our premortal existence. It was the culture of Adam and Enoch. It was the culture founded on the Savior's teachings in the meridian of time, and it is available to all women and men once again in our day. It is unique. It is the greatest of all cultures and comes from the great plan of happiness, authored by God and championed by Christ. It unites rather than divides. It heals rather than harms.

The gospel of Jesus Christ teaches us that there is purpose in life. Our being here is not just some big cosmic accident or mistake! We are here for a reason.

This culture is grounded in the testimony that our Heavenly Father exists, that He is real and loves each one of us individually. We are His "work and [His] glory."[1] This culture espouses the concept of equal worth. There is no recognition of caste or class. We are, after all, brothers and sisters, spirit children of our heavenly parents—literally. There is no prejudice or "us versus them" mentality in the greatest of all cultures. We are all "us." We are all "them." We believe that we are responsible and accountable for ourselves, one another, the Church, and our world. Responsibility and accountability are important factors in our growth.

Charity, true Christlike caring, is the bedrock of this culture. We feel real concern for the needs of our fellowman, temporal and spiritual, and act on those feelings. This dispels prejudice and hatred.

We enjoy a culture of revelation, centered on the word of God as received by the prophets (and personally verifiable to each one of us through the Holy Ghost). All humankind can know the will and mind of God.

This culture champions the principle of agency. The ability to choose is extremely important for our development and our happiness. Choosing wisely is essential.

It is a culture of learning and study. We seek knowledge and wisdom and the best in all things.

It is a culture of faith and obedience. Faith in Jesus Christ is the first principle of our culture, and obedience to His teachings and commandments is the outcome. These give rise to self-mastery.

It is a culture of prayer. We believe that God will not only hear us but also help us.

It is a culture of covenants and ordinances, high moral standards, sacrifice, forgiveness and repentance, and caring for the temple of our bodies. All of these bear witness to our commitment to God.

It is a culture governed by the priesthood, the authority to act in God's name, the power of God to bless His children. It edifies and enables individuals to be better people, leaders, mothers, fathers, and companions—and it sanctifies the home.

True miracles abound in this, the oldest of all cultures, wrought by faith in Jesus Christ, the power of the priesthood, prayer, self-improvement, true conversion, and forgiveness.

It is a culture of missionary work. The worth of souls is great.

In the culture of Christ, women are elevated to their proper and eternal status. They are not subservient to men, as in many cultures in today's world, but full and equal partners here and in the world to come.

This culture sanctions the sanctity of the family. The family is the basic unit of eternity. The perfection of the family is worth any sacrifice because, as has been taught, "no other success can compensate for failure in the home."[2] The home is where our best work is done and where our greatest happiness is attained.

In the culture of Christ, there is perspective—and eternal focus and direction. This culture is concerned with things of lasting worth! It comes from the gospel of Jesus Christ, which is eternal and explains the why, what, and where of our existence. (It is inclusive, not exclusive.) Because this culture results from the application of our Savior's teachings, it helps provide a healing balm of which our world is in such desperate need.

What a blessing it is to be part of this grand and noble way of life! To be part of this, the greatest of all cultures, will require change. The prophets have taught that it is necessary to leave behind anything in our old cultures that is inconsistent with the culture of Christ. But that doesn't mean we have to leave behind *everything.* The prophets have also emphasized that we are invited, one and all, to bring our faith and talents and knowledge—all that is good in our lives and our individual cultures—*with* us and let the Church "add to it" through the message of the gospel.[3]

The Church of Jesus Christ of Latter-day Saints is hardly a Western society or an American cultural phenomenon. It is an international church, as it was always meant to be. More than that, it is supernal. New members from around the world bring richness, diversity, and excitement into our ever-growing family. Latter-day Saints everywhere still celebrate and honor their own heritage and heroes, but now they are also part of something far grander. The culture of Christ helps us to see ourselves as we really are, and when seen through the lens of eternity, tempered with righteousness, it serves to increase our ability to fulfill the great plan of happiness.

So what happened to my friend? Well, he was taught the lessons and joined the Church. His family has since been sealed for time and all eternity in the Sydney Australia Temple. He has given up little—and gained the potential for everything. He discovered that he can still celebrate his history, still be proud of his ancestry, his music and dance and literature, his food, his land and its people. He has found that there is no problem incorporating the best of his local culture into the greatest of all cultures. He discovered that bringing that which is consistent with truth and righteousness from his old life into his new one serves only to enhance his fellowship with the Saints and to assist in uniting all as one in the society of heaven.

We can, indeed, all cherish the best of our individual earthly cultures and still be full participants in the oldest culture of them all—the original, the ultimate, the eternal culture that comes from the gospel of Jesus Christ. What a marvelous heritage we all share. In the name of Jesus Christ, amen.

Notes

1. Moses 1:39.
2. J. E. McCulloch, in *Teachings of Presidents of the Church: David O. McKay* (2011), 154.
3. See *Teachings of Presidents of the Church: George Albert Smith* (2011), xxviii; Gordon B. Hinckley, "The Marvelous Foundation of Our Faith," *Ensign* or *Liahona*, Nov. 2002, 78–81.

GOD WILL DO SOMETHING UNIMAGINABLE

ELDER DIETER F. UCHTDORF

Of the Quorum of the Twelve Apostles

Not long after arriving in the Salt Lake Valley, the Latter-day Saints began building their holy temple. They felt they had finally found a place where they could worship God in peace and be free from persecution.

However, just as the temple foundation was nearing completion, an army of United States soldiers approached to forcibly install a new governor.

Because Church leaders did not know how hostile the army would be, Brigham Young ordered the Saints to evacuate and bury the temple foundation.

I'm sure some members of the Church wondered why their efforts to build God's kingdom were constantly being frustrated.

Eventually, the danger passed, and the temple foundations were excavated and inspected. It was then that the pioneer builders discovered that some of the original sandstones had cracked, making them unsuitable as a foundation.

Consequently, Brigham had them repair the foundation so that it could adequately support the granite[1] walls of the majestic Salt Lake Temple.[2] Finally, the Saints could sing the hymn "How Firm a Foundation"[3] and know their holy temple was built on a solid foundation that would last for generations.

This story can teach us how God uses adversity to bring about His purposes.

A Worldwide Pandemic

If this sounds familiar given the circumstances in which we find ourselves today, it's because it is.

I doubt there is a person who hears my voice or reads my words who has not been affected by the worldwide pandemic.

To those who mourn the loss of family and friends, we mourn

with you. We plead with Heavenly Father to comfort and console you.

The long-term consequences of this virus go beyond physical health. Many families have lost incomes and are threatened with hunger, uncertainty, and apprehension. We admire the selfless efforts of so many to prevent the spread of this disease. We are humbled by the quiet sacrifice and noble efforts of those who have risked their own safety to assist, heal, and support people in need. Our hearts are full of gratitude for your goodness and compassion.

We pray mightily that God will open the windows of heaven and fill your lives with God's eternal blessings.

We Are Seeds

There are still a lot of unknowns about this virus. But if there is one thing I do know, it is that this virus did not catch Heavenly Father by surprise. He did not have to muster additional battalions of angels, call emergency meetings, or divert resources from the world-creation division to handle an unexpected need.

My message today is that even though this pandemic is not what we wanted or expected, God has prepared His children and His Church for this time.

We will endure this, yes. But we will do more than simply grit our teeth, hold on, and wait for things to return to the old normal. We will move forward, and we will be better as a result.

In a way, we are seeds. And for seeds to reach their potential, they must be buried before they can sprout. It is my witness that though at times we may feel buried by the trials of life or surrounded by emotional darkness, the love of God and the blessings of the restored gospel of Jesus Christ will bring something unimaginable to spring forth.

Blessings Come from Hardship

Every dispensation has faced its times of trial and hardship.

Enoch and his people lived in a time of wickedness, wars, and bloodshed. "But the Lord came and dwelt with his people." He had something unimaginable in mind for them. He helped them establish Zion—a people "of one heart and one mind" who "dwelt in righteousness."[4]

Young Joseph, the son of Jacob, was thrown into a pit, sold into slavery, betrayed, and abandoned.[5] Joseph must have wondered if God had forgotten him. God had something unimaginable in mind for Joseph. He used this period of trial to strengthen Joseph's character and put him in a position to save his family.[6]

Think of Joseph Smith the Prophet while imprisoned in Liberty Jail, how he pled for relief for the suffering Saints. He must have wondered how Zion could be established in those circumstances. But the Lord spoke peace to him, and the glorious revelation that followed brought peace to the Saints—and it continues to bring peace to you and me.[7]

How many times in the early years of The Church of Jesus Christ of Latter-day Saints did the Saints despair and wonder if God had forgotten them? But through persecutions, perils, and threats of extermination, the Lord God of Israel had something else in mind for His little flock. Something unimaginable.

What do we learn from these examples—and the hundreds of others in the scriptures?

First, the righteous are not given a free pass that allows them to avoid the valleys of shadow. We all must walk through difficult times, for it is in these times of adversity that we learn principles that fortify our characters and cause us to draw closer to God.

Second, our Heavenly Father knows that we suffer, and because we are His children, He will not abandon us.[8]

Think of the compassionate one, the Savior, who spent so much of His life ministering to the sick, the lonely, the doubting, the despairing.[9] Do you think He is any less concerned about you today?

My dear friends, my beloved brothers and sisters, God will watch over and shepherd you during these times of uncertainty and fear. He knows you. He hears your pleas. He is faithful and dependable. He will fulfill His promises.

God has something unimaginable in mind for you personally and the Church collectively—a marvelous work and a wonder.

We Thank Thee, O God, for a Prophet

Our best days are ahead of us, not behind us. This is why God gives us *modern* revelation! Without it, life might feel like flying in a holding pattern, waiting for the fog to lift so we can land safely. The Lord's purposes for us are much higher than that. Because this is the Church of the living Christ, and because He directs His prophets, we are moving forward and upward to places we've never been, to heights we can hardly imagine!

Now, this does not mean we won't experience turbulence in our flight through mortality. It doesn't mean there won't be unexpected instrument failures, mechanical malfunctions, or serious weather challenges. In fact, things might get worse before they get better.

As a fighter pilot and airline captain, I learned that while I could not choose the adversity I would encounter during a flight, I could choose how I prepared and how I reacted. What is needed during times of crisis is calm and clear-headed trust.

How do we do this?

We face the facts and return to the fundamentals, to the basic gospel principles, to what matters most. You strengthen your private religious behavior—like prayer and scripture study and keeping God's commandments. You make the decisions based on best proven practices.

Focus on the things you can do and not on the things you cannot do.

You muster your faith. And you listen for the guiding word of the Lord and His prophet to lead you to safety.

Remember, this is the Church of Jesus Christ—He is at the helm.

Think of the many inspired advancements that happened in the past decade alone. To mention just a few:

- The sacrament was reemphasized as center of our Sabbath worship.

- *Come, Follow Me* was provided as a home-centered, Church-supported tool to strengthen individuals and families.
- We began a higher and holier way of ministering to all.
- The use of technology in sharing the gospel and doing the Lord's work has spread throughout the Church.

Even these general conference sessions would not be possible without the wonderful tools of technology.

Brothers and sisters, with Christ at the helm, things will not only be all right; they will be unimaginable.

The Work of Gathering Israel Goes Forward

At first it may have seemed that a worldwide pandemic would be a roadblock to the Lord's work. For example, traditional methods of sharing the gospel have not been possible. However, the pandemic is revealing new and more creative ways of reaching out to the honest in heart. The work of gathering Israel is increasing in power and enthusiasm. Hundreds and thousands of stories attest to this.

A good friend living in beautiful Norway wrote to Harriet and me about a recent increase in baptisms. "In locations where the Church is small," she wrote, "twigs will become branches, and branches will become wards!!"

In Latvia, a woman who had discovered the Church by clicking on an internet ad was so excited to learn about the gospel of Jesus Christ that she showed up to her appointment an hour early, and before the missionaries ended the first lesson, she asked for a date to be baptized.

In Eastern Europe, one woman who received a call from the missionaries exclaimed, "Sisters, why haven't you called earlier? I've been waiting!"

Many of our missionaries are busier than ever. Many are teaching more people than ever. There is an increased connection between members and missionaries.

In the past, we might have been so tied to traditional approaches that it took a pandemic to open our eyes. Perhaps we were still building with sandstone when granite was already available. Of necessity, we are now learning how to use a variety of methods, including technology, to invite people—in normal and natural ways—to come and see, come and help, and come and belong.

His Work, His Ways

This is the Lord's work. He invites us to find His ways of doing it, and they may differ from our past experiences.

This happened to Simon Peter and other disciples who went fishing on the Sea of Tiberias.

"That night they caught nothing.

"But when the morning [came], Jesus stood on the shore. . . .

"And he said unto them, Cast the net on the [*other*] side of the ship, and ye shall find."

They did cast their nets on the other side and "were not able to draw it for the multitude of fishes."[10]

God has revealed and will continue to reveal His almighty hand. The day will come when we will look back and know that during this time of adversity, God was helping us to find better ways—His ways—to build His kingdom on a firm foundation.

I bear my witness that this is God's work and He will continue to do many unimaginable things among His children, His people. God holds us in the palm of His caring and compassionate hands.

I testify that President Russell M. Nelson is God's prophet for our day.

As an Apostle of the Lord, I invite and bless you to "cheerfully do all things that lie in [your] power; and then may [you] stand still, with the utmost assurance, to see the salvation of God, and for his arm to be revealed."[11] And I promise that the Lord will cause unimaginable things to come from your righteous labors. In the name of Jesus Christ, amen.

Notes

1. Quartz monzonite that looked like granite, taken from a quarry at the mouth of Little Cottonwood Canyon, 20 miles (32 km) southeast of the city.
2. For a more in-depth look at this period of history, see *Saints: The Story of the Church of Jesus Christ in the Latter Days*, vol. 2, *No Unhallowed Hand, 1846–1893* (2020), chapters 17, 19, and 21.
3. See "How Firm a Foundation," *Hymns*, no. 85.

The verses of this great anthem can serve as a theme for our times, and when we listen to the lyrics with new ears, it provides insight into the challenges we face:

In ev'ry condition—in sickness, in health,
In poverty's vale or abounding in wealth,
At home or abroad, on the land or the sea—
As thy days may demand, . . . so thy succor shall be.
Fear not, I am with thee; oh, be not dismayed,
For I am thy God and will still give thee aid.
I'll strengthen thee, help thee, and cause thee to stand,
Upheld by my righteous, . . . omnipotent hand.
When through the deep waters I call thee to go,
The rivers of sorrow shall not thee o'erflow,
For I will be with thee, thy troubles to bless,
And sanctify to thee . . . thy deepest distress.
When through fiery trials thy pathway shall lie,
My grace, all sufficient, shall be thy supply.
The flame shall not hurt thee; I only design
Thy dross to consume . . . and thy gold to refine. . . .
The soul that on Jesus hath leaned for repose
I will not, I cannot, desert to his foes;
That soul, though all hell should endeavor to shake,
I'll never, no never, . . . no never forsake!

4. See Moses 7:13–18.
5. Joseph was perhaps as young as 17 when his brothers sold him into slavery (see Genesis 37:2). He was 30 years old when he entered Pharaoh's service (see Genesis 41:46). Can you imagine how difficult it was for a young man in his prime to be betrayed, sold into slavery, falsely accused, and then imprisoned? Joseph certainly is a model for not only the youth of the Church but also every man, woman, and child who desires to take up the cross and follow the Savior.
6. See Genesis 45:4–11; 50:20–21. In Psalm 105:17–18, we read, "He sent a man before them, even Joseph, who was sold for a servant: whose feet they hurt with fetters: he was laid in iron." In another translation, verse 18 reads, "They have afflicted with fetters his feet, Iron hath entered his soul" (Young's Literal Translation). To me, this suggests that Joseph's hardships gave him a soul as strong and resilient as iron—a quality he would need for the great and unimaginable future the Lord had in store for him.
7. See Doctrine and Covenants 121–23.
8. If God commands His children to be aware of and compassionate toward the hungry, the needy, the naked, the sick, and the afflicted, surely He will be aware and merciful to us, His children (see Mormon 8:39).
9. See Luke 7:11–17.
10. See John 21:1–6.
11. Doctrine and Covenants 123:17.

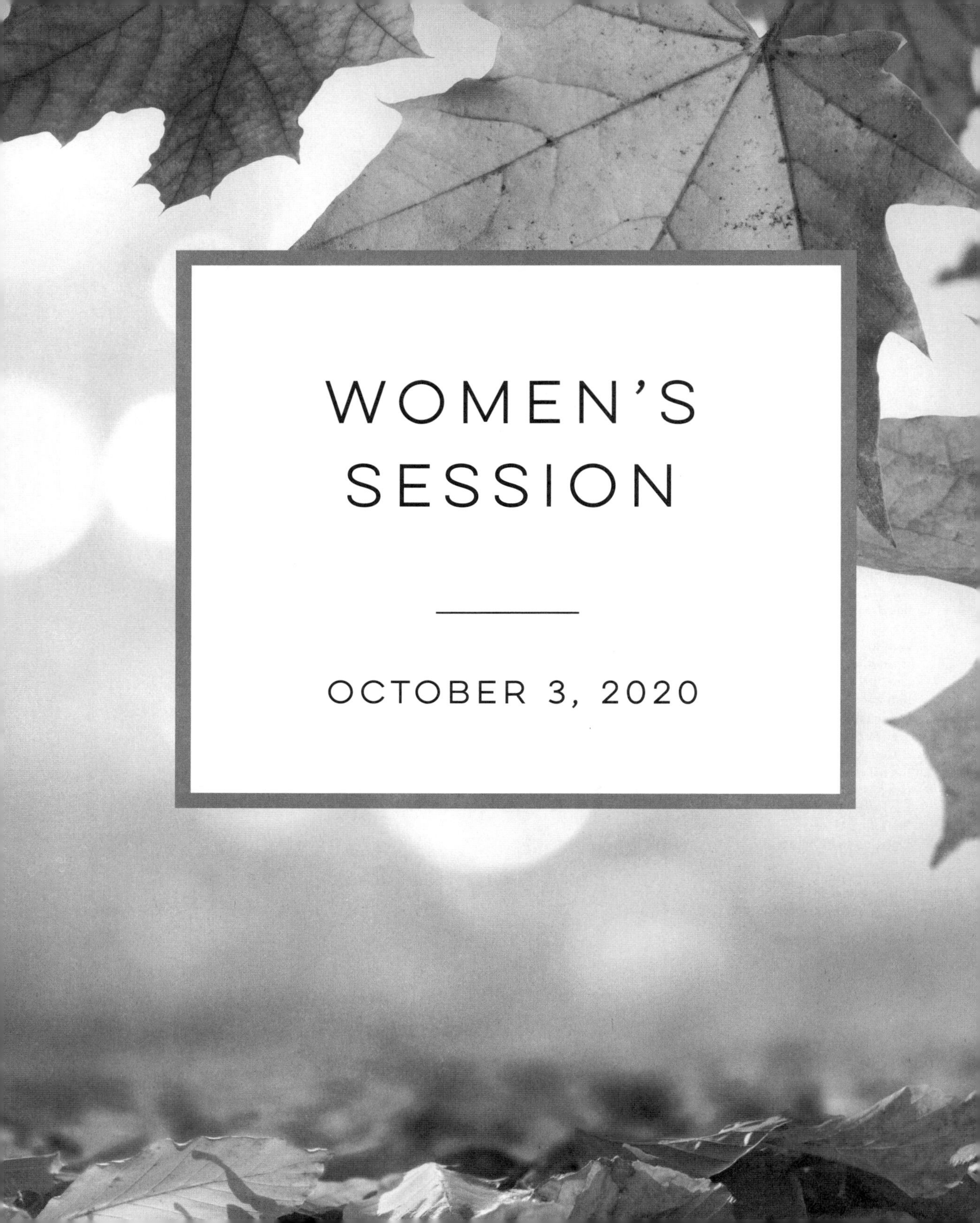

WOMEN'S SESSION

OCTOBER 3, 2020

BY UNION OF FEELING WE OBTAIN POWER WITH GOD

SHARON EUBANK
First Counselor in the Relief Society General Presidency

Gordon's mother told him if he would finish his chores, she would make him a pie. His favorite kind. Just for him. Gordon went to work on getting those chores done, and his mother rolled out the pie. His older sister Kathy came into the house with a friend. She saw the pie and asked if she and her friend could have a slice.

"No," said Gordon, "it's my pie. Mom baked it for me, and I had to earn it."

Kathy snapped at her little brother. He was so self-centered and ungenerous. How could he keep this all to himself?

Hours later when Kathy opened the car door to take her friend home, there on the seat were two napkins folded nicely, two forks set on top, and two wide pieces of pie on plates. Kathy told this story at Gordon's funeral to show how he was willing to change and show kindness to those who didn't always deserve it.

In 1842, the Saints were working hard to build the Nauvoo Temple. After the founding of the Relief Society in March, the Prophet Joseph often came to their meetings to prepare them for the sacred, unifying covenants they would soon make in the temple.

On June 9, the Prophet "said he was going to preach mercy[.] Supposing that Jesus Christ and [the] angels should object to us on frivolous things, what would become of us? We must be merciful and overlook small things." President Smith continued, "It grieves me that there is no fuller fellowship—if one member suffer all feel it—by union of feeling we obtain pow'r with God."[1]

That small sentence struck me like lightning. *By union of feeling we obtain power with God.* This world isn't what I want it to be. There are many things I want to influence and make better. And frankly, there is a lot of opposition to what I hope for, and sometimes I feel powerless. Lately, I have been asking myself searching questions: How can I understand people around me better? How will I create that "union of feeling" when all are so different? What power from God might I access if I am just a little bit more unified with others? From my soul-searching, I have three suggestions. Maybe they will help you too.

Have Mercy

Jacob 2:17 reads, "Think of your [brothers and sisters] like unto yourselves, and be familiar with all and free with your substance, that they may be rich like unto you." Let's replace the word *substance* with *mercy*—be free with your *mercy* that they may be rich like unto you.

We often think of substance in terms of food or money, but perhaps what we all need more of in our ministering is mercy.

My own Relief Society president recently said: "The thing I . . . promise . . . you is that I will keep your name safe. . . . I will see you for who you are at your best. . . . I will never say anything about you that is unkind, that is not going to lift you. I ask you to do the same for me because I am terrified, frankly, of letting you down."

Joseph Smith told the sisters on that June day in 1842:

"When persons manifest the least kindness and love to me, O what pow'r it has over my mind. . . .

". . . The nearer we get to our heavenly Father, the more are we dispos'd to look with compassion on perishing souls—[we feel that we want] to take them upon our shoulders and cast their sins behind our back. [My talk is intended for] all this Society—if you would have God have mercy on you, have mercy on one another."[2]

This was counsel specifically to the Relief Society. Let's not judge each other or let our words bite. Let's keep each other's names safe and give the gift of mercy.[3]

Make Your Boat *Swing*

In 1936, an obscure rowing team from the University of Washington traveled to Germany to participate in the Olympic Games. It was the depths of the Great Depression. These were working-class boys whose small mining and lumber towns donated bits of money so they could travel to Berlin. Every aspect of the competition seemed stacked against them, but something happened in the race. In the rowing world, they call it "swing." Listen to this description based on the book *The Boys in the Boat:*

There is a thing that sometimes happens that is hard to achieve and hard to define. It's called "swing." It happens only when all are rowing in such perfect unison that not a single action is out of sync.

Rowers must rein in their fierce independence and at the same time hold true to their individual capabilities. Races are not won by clones. Good crews are good blends—someone to lead the charge, someone to hold something in reserve, someone to fight the fight, someone to make peace. No rower is more valuable than another, all are assets to the boat, but if they are to row well together, each must adjust to the needs and capabilities of the others—the shorter-armed person reaching a little farther, the longer-armed person pulling in just a bit.

Differences can be turned to advantage instead of disadvantage. Only then will it feel as if the boat is moving on its own. Only then does pain entirely give way to exultation. Good "swing" feels like poetry.[4]

Against towering obstacles, this team found perfect swing and won. The Olympic gold was exhilarating, but the unity each rower experienced that day was a holy moment that stayed with them all their lives.

Clear Away the Bad as Fast as the Good Can Grow

In the exquisite allegory in Jacob 5, the Lord of the vineyard planted a good tree in good ground, but it became corrupted over time and brought forth wild fruit. The Lord of the vineyard says eight times: "It grieveth me [to] lose this tree."

The servant says to the Lord of the vineyard: "Spare [the tree] a little longer. And the Lord said: Yea, I will spare it a little longer."[5]

And then comes instruction that can be applied to all of us trying to dig about and find good fruit in our own little vineyards: "Ye shall clear away the bad according as the good shall grow."[6]

Unity doesn't magically happen; it takes work. It's messy, sometimes uncomfortable, and happens gradually when we clear away the bad as fast as the good can grow.

We are never alone in our efforts to create unity. Jacob 5 continues, "The servants did go and labor with their mights; and the Lord of the vineyard labored also with them."[7]

Each of us is going to have deeply wounding experiences, things that should never happen. Each of us will also, at various times, allow pride and loftiness to corrupt the fruit we bear. But Jesus Christ is our Savior in all things. His power reaches to the very bottom and is reliably there for us when we call on Him. We all beg for mercy for our sins and failures. He freely gives it. And He asks us if we can give that same mercy and understanding to each other.

Jesus put it bluntly: "Be one; and if ye are not one ye are not mine."[8] But if we are one—if we can spare a piece of our pie or fit our individual talents so the boat can swing in perfect unison—then we are His. And He will help clear away the bad as fast as the good does grow.

Prophetic Promises

We may not yet be where we want to be, and we are not now where we will be. I believe the change we seek in ourselves and in the groups we belong to will come less by activism and more by actively trying every day to understand one another. Why? Because we are building Zion—a people "of one heart and one mind."[9]

As covenant women, we have broad influence. That influence is applied in everyday moments when we are studying with a friend, putting children to bed, talking to a seatmate on the bus, preparing a presentation with a colleague. We have power to remove prejudice and build unity.

Relief Society and Young Women are not simply classes. They can also be unforgettable experiences where very different women all get into the same boat and row until we find our *swing*. I offer this invitation: be part of a collective force that changes the world for good. Our covenantal assignment is to minister, to lift up the hands that hang down, to put struggling people on our backs or in our arms and carry them. It isn't complicated to know what to do, but it often goes against our selfish interests, and we have to try. The women of this Church have unlimited potential to change society. I have full spiritual confidence that, as we seek union of feeling, we will call down the power of God to make our efforts whole.

When the Church commemorated the 1978 revelation on priesthood, President Russell M. Nelson extended a powerful prophetic blessing: "It is my prayer *and blessing* that I leave upon all who are listening that we may overcome any burdens of prejudice and walk uprightly with God—and with one another—in perfect peace and harmony."[10]

May we draw on this prophetic blessing and use our individual and collective efforts to increase unity in the world. I leave my testimony in the words of the Lord Jesus Christ's humble, timeless prayer: "That they all may be one; as thou, Father, art in me, and I in thee, that they also may be one in us."[11] In the name of Jesus Christ, amen.

Notes

1. "Minutes and Discourse, 9 June 1842," 61, Joseph Smith Papers, josephsmithpapers.org/paper-summary/minutes-and-discourse-9-june-1842/1.
2. "Minutes and Discourse, 9 June 1842," 62, Joseph Smith Papers, josephsmithpapers.org/paper-summary/minutes-and-discourse-9-june-1842/2.
3. See Cree-L Kofford, "Your Name Is Safe in Our Home," *Ensign*, May 1999, 81–83; *Liahona*, July 1999, 96–98.
4. See Daniel James Brown, *The Boys in the Boat: Nine Americans and Their Epic Quest for Gold at the 1936 Berlin Olympics* (2013), 161, 179.
5. Jacob 5:50–51.
6. Jacob 5:66.
7. Jacob 5:72.
8. Doctrine and Covenants 38:27.
9. Moses 7:18.
10. Russell M. Nelson, "Building Bridges," *New Era*, Aug. 2018, 6; *Liahona*, Dec. 2018, 51; emphasis added.
11. John 17:21.

KEEP THE CHANGE

BECKY CRAVEN

Second Counselor in the Young Women General Presidency

Imagine someone going to a market to purchase an item. If she pays the cashier more than the item is worth, the cashier will give her change.

King Benjamin taught his people in ancient America of the tremendous blessings we receive from our Savior, Jesus Christ. He created the heavens, the earth, and all the beauty we enjoy.[1] Through His loving Atonement, He provides a way for us to be redeemed from sin and death.[2] As we show our gratitude to Him by diligently living His commandments, He immediately blesses us, leaving us always in His debt.

He gives us much, much more than the value of what we can ever return to Him. So, what can we give to Him, who paid the incalculable price for our sins? We can give Him *change.* We can give Him our *change.* It may be a change of thought, a change in habit, or a change in the direction we are headed. In return for His priceless payment for each of us, the Lord asks us for a change of heart. The change He requests from us is not for His benefit but for ours. So, unlike the purchaser at the market who would take back the change we offer, our gracious Savior beckons us to *keep the change.*

After hearing the words spoken by King Benjamin, his people cried out, declaring that their hearts had changed, saying, "Because of the Spirit of the Lord Omnipotent, which has wrought a mighty change in us, . . . we have no more disposition to do evil, but to do good continually."[3] The scriptures do not say that they immediately became perfect; rather, their desire to change compelled them to action. Their change of heart meant putting off the natural man or woman and yielding to the Spirit as they strove to become more like Jesus Christ.

President Henry B. Eyring teaches: "True conversion depends on seeking freely in faith, with great effort and some pain. Then it is the Lord who can grant . . . the miracle of cleansing and change."[4]

Combining our effort with the Savior's ability to change us, we become new creatures.

When I was younger, I visualized myself walking along an upward, vertical path toward my goal of eternal life. Each time I did or said something wrong, I felt myself sliding down the path, only to start my journey all over again. It was like landing on that one square in the children's game Chutes and Ladders that slides you down from the top of the board back to the beginning of the game! It was discouraging! But as I began to understand the doctrine of Christ[5] and how to apply it daily in my life, I found hope.

Jesus Christ has given us a continuous pattern for change. He invites us to exercise faith in Him, which inspires us to repent—"which faith and repentance bringeth a change of heart."[6] As we repent and turn our hearts to Him, we gain a greater desire to make and live sacred covenants. We endure to the end by continuing to apply these principles throughout our lives and inviting the Lord to change us. Enduring to the end means *changing* to the end. I now understand that I am not starting over with each failed attempt, but that with each try, I am continuing my process of change.

There is an inspired phrase in the Young Women theme that states, "I cherish the gift of repentance and seek to improve each day."[7] I pray that we do cherish this beautiful gift and that we are intentional in seeking change. Sometimes the changes we need to make are associated with serious sin. But most often, we strive to refine our character to align ourselves with the attributes of Jesus Christ. Our daily choices will either help or hinder our progress. Small but steady, deliberate changes will help us improve. Do not become discouraged. Change is a lifelong process. I am grateful that in our struggles to change, the Lord is patient with us.

Through Jesus Christ, we are given the strength to make lasting changes. As we humbly turn to Him, He will increase our capacity to change.

In addition to the transforming power of our Savior's Atonement, the Holy Ghost will support and guide us as we put forth our effort. He can even help us know what changes we need to make.

We can also find help and encouragement through priesthood blessings, prayer, fasting, and attending the temple.

Likewise, trusted family members, leaders, and friends can be helpful in our efforts to change. When I was eight years old, my older brother, Lee, and I would spend time with our friends playing in the branches of a neighborhood tree. We loved being together in the fellowship of our friends in the shade of that tree. One day, Lee fell out of the tree and broke his arm. Having a broken arm made it hard for him to climb the tree by himself. But life in the tree just wasn't the same without him there. So some of us steadied him from behind while others pulled on his good arm, and without too much effort, Lee was back in the tree. His arm was still broken, but he was with us again, enjoying our friendship as he healed.

I have often thought about my experience of playing in the tree as being a type of our activity in the gospel of Jesus Christ. In the shade of gospel branches, we enjoy many blessings associated with our covenants. Some may have fallen from the safety of their covenants and need our help climbing back into the security of gospel branches. It can be difficult for them to come back on their own. Can we gently tug a little here and hoist up a little there to help them heal while they enjoy our friendship?

If you are suffering an injury from a fall, please allow others to help you return to your covenants and the blessings they offer. The Savior can help you heal and change while surrounded by those who love you.

I occasionally run into friends whom I haven't seen for many years. Sometimes they say, "You haven't changed at all!" Each time I hear that, I cringe a little, because I hope *I have changed* over the years. I hope I have changed since yesterday! I hope I am a little kinder, less judgmental, and more compassionate. I hope I am quicker to respond to the needs of others, and I hope I am just a little bit more patient.

I love hiking in the mountains near my home. Often, I get a little rock in my shoe as I walk along the trail. Eventually, I stop and shake out my shoe. But it astounds me how long I allow myself to hike in pain before I stop and rid myself of the irritant.

As we travel the covenant path, sometimes we pick up stones in our shoes in the form of poor habits, sins, or bad attitudes. The quicker we shake them from our lives, the more joyful our mortal journey will be.

Maintaining change takes effort. I cannot imagine stopping along the trail only to put back in my shoe the annoying and painful pebble I just removed. I would not want to do that any more than a beautiful butterfly would choose to return to her cocoon.

I testify that because of Jesus Christ, we *can* change. We can adjust our habits, alter our thoughts, and refine our character to become more like Him. And with His help, we can *keep the change.* In the name of Jesus Christ, amen.

Notes

1. See Mosiah 4:9.
2. See Mosiah 3:5–12.
3. Mosiah 5:2.
4. Henry B. Eyring, "We Must Raise Our Sights," *Ensign*, Sept. 2004, 18.
5. See 2 Nephi 31:21; 3 Nephi 27:13–21.
6. Helaman 15:7.
7. Young Women theme, ChurchofJesusChrist.org.

THE HEALING POWER OF JESUS CHRIST

CRISTINA B. FRANCO

Second Counselor in the Primary General Presidency

Since the beginning of this year, we have dealt with many unexpected events. The loss of life and income due to the worldwide pandemic has seriously affected the global community and economy.

Earthquakes, fires, and floods in different parts of the world, as well as other weather-related disasters, have left people feeling helpless, hopeless, and brokenhearted, wondering if their lives will ever be the same.

Let me tell you a personal story about brokenness.

When our children were young, they decided they wanted to take piano lessons. My husband, Rudy, and I wanted to provide our children this opportunity, but we had no piano. We could not afford a new piano, so Rudy started looking for a used one.

That year for Christmas, he surprised us all with a piano, and through the years, our children learned to play.

When our sons grew up and left the house, the old piano just collected dust, so we sold it. A few years went by, and we had saved some money. One day Rudy said, "I think it's time we get a new piano."

I asked, "Why would we get a new piano, when neither of us plays?"

He said, "Oh, but we can get a piano that plays itself! By using an iPad, you can program the piano to play over 4,000 songs, including hymns, Tabernacle Choir songs, all the Primary songs, and so many more."

Rudy is a great salesperson, to say the least.

We purchased a beautiful new player piano, and a few days later, two big, strong men delivered it to our house.

I showed them where I wanted it and moved out of the way.

It was a heavy baby grand, and to fit it through the door, they removed the legs and managed to put the piano sideways on top of a moving dolly that they had brought with them.

Our house sat on a little bit of a slope, and unfortunately earlier that day it had snowed, leaving things wet and slushy. Can you see where this is going?

While the men were moving the piano up the little slope, it slipped, and I heard a big, loud crash. The piano had fallen off the moving dolly and hit the ground so hard that it left a big dent in our lawn.

I said, "Oh, my goodness. Are you OK?"

Thankfully both men were OK.

Their eyes were wide as they looked at each other, then looked at me and said, "We are so sorry. We'll take it back to the store and have our manager call you."

Soon the manager was talking with Rudy to arrange delivery of a new piano. Rudy is kind and forgiving and told the manager it was OK if they just repaired the damage and brought back the same piano, but the manager insisted on getting us a new one.

Rudy responded, saying, "It couldn't be that bad. Just fix it up and bring it over."

The manager said, "The wood is broken, and once the wood is broken, it can never sound the same. You will get a new piano."

Sisters and brothers, aren't we all like this piano, a little broken, cracked, and damaged, feeling like we will never be the same again? However, as we come unto Jesus Christ by exercising faith in Him, repenting, and making and keeping covenants, our brokenness —whatever its cause—can be healed. This process, which invites the Savior's healing power into our lives, does not just restore us to what we were before but makes us better than we ever were. I know that through our Savior, Jesus Christ, we can all be mended, made whole, and fulfill our purpose, just like a beautiful-sounding, brand-new piano.

President Russell M. Nelson taught: "When sore trials come upon us, it's time to deepen our faith in God, to work hard, and to serve others. Then He will heal our broken hearts. He will bestow upon us personal peace and comfort. Those great gifts will not be destroyed, even by death."[1]

Jesus said:

"Come unto me, all ye that labour and are heavy laden, and I will give you rest.

"Take my yoke upon you, and learn of me; for I am meek and lowly in heart: and ye shall find rest unto your souls.

"For my yoke is easy, and my burden is light" (Matthew 11:28–30).

To heal brokenness by coming unto Him, we need to have faith in Jesus Christ. "Having faith in Jesus Christ means relying completely on Him—trusting in His infinite power . . . and love. It includes believing His teachings. It means believing that even though we do not understand all things, He does. Because He has experienced all our pains, afflictions, and infirmities, He knows how to help us rise above our daily difficulties."[2]

As we come unto Him, "we can be filled with joy, peace, and consolation. All that is [hard and challenging] about life can be made right through the Atonement of Jesus Christ."[3] He has counseled us, "Look unto me in every thought; doubt not, fear not" (Doctrine and Covenants 6:36).

In the Book of Mormon when Alma and his people were nearly crushed by the burdens placed upon them, the people pleaded for relief. The Lord didn't take away their burdens; instead He promised them:

"And I will also ease the burdens which are put upon your shoulders, that even you cannot feel them upon your backs, even while you are in bondage; and this will I do that ye may stand as witnesses for me hereafter, and that ye may know of a surety that I, the Lord God, do visit my people in their afflictions.

"And now it came to pass that the burdens which were laid upon Alma and his brethren were made light; yea, the Lord did strengthen them that they could bear up their burdens with ease, and they did submit cheerfully and with patience to all the will of the Lord" (Mosiah 24:14–15).

Of the Savior's ability to heal and lighten burdens, Elder Tad R. Callister has taught:

"One of the blessings of the Atonement is that we can receive of the Savior's succoring powers. Isaiah spoke repeatedly of the Lord's healing, calming influence. He testified that the Savior was 'a strength to the needy in his distress, a refuge from the storm, a shadow from the heat' (Isaiah 25:4). As to those who sorrow, Isaiah declared that the Savior possessed the power to 'comfort all that mourn' (Isaiah 61:2), and 'wipe away tears from off all faces' (Isaiah 25:8; see also Revelation 7:17); 'revive the spirit of the humble' (Isaiah 57:15); and 'bind up the brokenhearted' (Isaiah 61:1; see also Luke 4:18; Psalm 147:3). So expansive was his succoring power that he could exchange 'beauty for ashes, the oil of joy for mourning, the garment of praise for the spirit of heaviness' (Isaiah 61:3).

"Oh, what hope soars in those promises! . . . His spirit heals; it refines; it comforts; it breathes new life into hopeless hearts. It has the power to transform all that is ugly and vicious and worthless in life to something of supreme and glorious splendor. He has the power to convert the ashes of mortality to the beauties of eternity."[4]

I testify that Jesus Christ is our loving Savior, our Redeemer, the Master Healer, and our faithful friend. If we turn to Him, He will heal us and make us whole again. I testify this is His Church and He is preparing to return once again to reign with power and glory on this earth. In the name of Jesus Christ, amen.

Notes

1. Russell M. Nelson, "Jesus Christ—the Master Healer," *Ensign* or *Liahona*, Nov. 2005, 87.
2. "Faith in Jesus Christ," Gospel Topics, topics.ChurchofJesusChrist.org.
3. *Preach My Gospel: A Guide to Missionary Service*, rev. ed. (2018), 52, ChurchofJesusChrist.org.
4. Tad R. Callister, *The Infinite Atonement* (2000), 206–7.

SISTERS IN ZION

PRESIDENT HENRY B. EYRING

Second Counselor in the First Presidency

My beloved sisters, I am blessed to speak during this wonderful time in the world's history. Every day, we are approaching closer to the glorious moment when the Savior Jesus Christ will come to earth again. We know something of the terrible events that will precede His coming, yet our hearts swell with joy and confidence also knowing of the glorious promises that will be fulfilled before He returns.

As the beloved daughters of Heavenly Father, and as the daughters of the Lord Jesus Christ in His kingdom,[1] you will play a crucial part in the grand times ahead. We know that the Savior will come to a people who have been gathered and prepared to live as the people did in the city of Enoch. The people there were united in faith in Jesus Christ and had become so completely pure that they were taken up to heaven.

Here is the Lord's revealed description of what would happen to Enoch's people and what will happen in *this* last dispensation of the fulness of times:

"And the day shall come that the earth shall rest, but before that day the heavens shall be darkened, and a veil of darkness shall cover the earth; and the heavens shall shake, and also the earth; and great tribulations shall be among the children of men, *but my people will I preserve;*

"And righteousness will I send down out of heaven; and truth will I send forth *out of the earth,* to bear testimony of mine Only Begotten; his resurrection from the dead; yea, and also the resurrection of all men; and righteousness and truth will I cause to sweep the earth as with a flood, to gather out mine elect from the four quarters of the earth, unto a place which I shall prepare, an Holy City, that my people may gird up their loins, and be looking forth for the time of *my coming;* for *there* shall be my tabernacle, and it shall be called Zion, a New Jerusalem.

"And the Lord said unto Enoch: Then shalt thou and all thy city meet them there, and we will receive them into our bosom, and they shall see us; and we will fall upon their necks, and they shall fall upon our necks, and we will kiss each other;

"And *there* shall be mine abode, and it shall be Zion, which shall come forth out of all the creations which I have made; and for the space of a thousand years the earth shall rest."[2]

You sisters, your daughters, your granddaughters, and the women you have nurtured will be at the heart of creating that society of people who will join in glorious association with the Savior. You will be an essential force in the gathering of Israel and in the creation of a Zion people who will dwell in peace in the New Jerusalem.

The Lord has, through His prophets, made a promise to you. In the early days of the Relief Society, the Prophet Joseph Smith said to the sisters, "If you live up to your privileges, the angels cannot be restrained from being your *associates.*"[3]

That marvelous potential lies within you, and you are being prepared for it.

President Gordon B. Hinckley said:

"You sisters . . . do not hold a second place in our Father's plan for the eternal happiness and well-being of His children. You are an absolutely essential part of that plan.

"Without you the plan could not function. Without you the entire program would be frustrated. . . .

"Each of you is a daughter of God, endowed with a divine birthright."[4]

Our current prophet, President Russell M. Nelson, has given this description of the part you play in preparation for the Savior's coming:

"It would be impossible to measure the influence that . . . women have, not only on families but also on the Lord's Church, as wives, mothers, and grandmothers; as sisters and aunts; as teachers and leaders; and especially as exemplars and devout defenders of the faith.

"This has been true in every gospel dispensation since the days of Adam and Eve. Yet the women of *this* dispensation are distinct from the women of *any* other because this dispensation is distinct from any other. This distinction brings both privileges and responsibilities."[5]

This dispensation is distinct in that the Lord will lead us to become prepared to be like the city of Enoch. He has described through His apostles and prophets what that transformation to a Zion people will entail.

Elder Bruce R. McConkie taught:

"[Enoch's] was a day of wickedness and evil, a day of darkness and rebellion, a day of war and desolation, a day leading up to the cleansing of the earth by water.

"Enoch, however, was faithful. He 'saw the Lord,' and talked with him 'face to face' as one man speaks with another. (Moses 7:4.) The Lord sent him to cry repentance to the world, and commissioned him to 'baptize in the name of the Father and of the Son, which is full of grace and truth, and of the Holy Ghost, which beareth record of the Father and the Son.' (Moses 7:11.) Enoch made covenants and assembled a congregation of true believers, all of whom *became* so faithful that 'the Lord came and dwelt with his people, and they dwelt in righteousness,' and were blessed from on high. 'And the Lord called his people Zion, because they were of one heart and one mind, and dwelt in righteousness; and there was no poor among them.' (Moses 7:18.) . . .

"After the Lord called his people Zion, the scripture says that Enoch 'built a city that was called the City of Holiness, even Zion;' that Zion 'was taken up into heaven' where 'God received it into his own bosom;" and that "from thence went forth the saying, Zion is fled.' (Moses 7:19, 21, 69.) . . .

"This same Zion which was taken up into heaven shall return . . . when the Lord brings again Zion, and its inhabitants shall join with the new Jerusalem, which shall then be established."[6]

If the past is prologue, at the time of the Savior's coming, the daughters who are deeply committed to their covenants with God will be more than half of those who are prepared to welcome Him when He comes. But whatever the numbers, your contribution in creating unity among the people prepared for that Zion will be far greater than half.

I will tell you why I believe that will be so. The Book of Mormon gives an account of a Zion people. You remember that it was after they had been taught, loved, and blessed by the resurrected Savior that "there was no contention in the land, because of the love of God which did dwell in the hearts of the people."[7]

My experience has taught me that Heavenly Father's daughters have a gift to allay contention and to promote righteousness with their love of God and with the love of God they engender in those they serve.

I saw it in my youth when our tiny branch met in my childhood home. My brother and I were the only Aaronic Priesthood holders, my father the only Melchizedek Priesthood holder. The branch Relief Society president was a convert whose husband was unhappy with her Church service. The members were all older sisters without a priesthood holder in their homes. I watched my mother and those sisters love, lift, and care for each other unfailingly. I realize now that I was given an early glimpse of Zion.

My tutorial in the influence of faithful women continued in a small branch of the Church in Albuquerque, New Mexico. I watched the branch president's wife, the district president's wife, and the Relief Society president warm the heart of every newcomer and convert. The Sunday I left Albuquerque, after two years observing the influence of sisters there, the first stake was created. Now the Lord has placed a temple there.

I moved next to Boston, where I served in the district presidency that presided over little branches spread across two states. There were contentions that more than once were resolved by loving and forgiving women who helped soften hearts. The Sunday I left Boston, a member of the First Presidency organized the first stake in Massachusetts. There is a temple there now, close to where the district president once lived. He had been brought into Church activity and was later called to serve as a stake president and then as a mission president, influenced by a faithful and loving wife.

Sisters, you were given the blessing of being daughters of God with special gifts. You brought with you into mortal life a spiritual capacity to nurture others and to lift them higher toward the love and purity that will qualify them to live together in a Zion society. It is not by accident that the Relief Society, the first Church organization specifically for Heavenly Father's daughters, has as its motto "Charity Never Faileth."

Charity is the pure love of Christ. And it is faith in Him and the full effects of His infinite Atonement that will qualify you, and those you love and serve, for the supernal gift to live in that sociality of a long-looked-for and promised Zion. There you will be sisters in Zion, loved in person by the Lord and those you have blessed.

I testify that you are citizens of the Lord's kingdom on the earth. You are daughters of a loving Heavenly Father, who sent you into the world with unique gifts that you promised to use to bless others. I promise you that the Lord will lead you by the hand, through the Holy Ghost. He will go before your face as you help Him prepare His people to become His promised Zion. I so testify in the sacred name of Jesus Christ, amen.

Notes

1. See Doctrine and Covenants 25:1.
2. Moses 7:61–64; emphasis added.
3. *Teachings of Presidents of the Church: Joseph Smith* (2007), 454; emphasis added.
4. Gordon B. Hinckley, "Women of the Church," *Ensign*, Nov. 1996, 67.
5. Russell M. Nelson, "A Plea to My Sisters," *Ensign* or *Liahona*, Nov. 2015, 95–96; emphasis added.
6. Bruce R. McConkie, "Building Zion," *Tambuli*, Sept. 1977, 13; emphasis added.
7. 4 Nephi 1:15.

BE OF GOOD CHEER

PRESIDENT DALLIN H. OAKS

First Counselor in the First Presidency

In the final days of His mortal life, Jesus Christ told His Apostles of the persecutions and hardships they would suffer.[1] He concluded with this great assurance: "In the world ye shall have tribulation: but be of good cheer; I have overcome the world" (John 16:33). That is the Savior's message to all of our Heavenly Father's children. That is the ultimate good news for each of us in our mortal lives.

"Be of good cheer" was also a needed assurance in the world into which the resurrected Christ sent His Apostles. "We are troubled on every side," the Apostle Paul later told the Corinthians, "yet not distressed; we are perplexed, but not in despair; persecuted, but not forsaken; cast down, but not destroyed" (2 Corinthians 4:8–9).

Two thousand years later we are also "troubled on every side," and we also need that same message not to despair but to be of good cheer. The Lord has special love and concern for His precious daughters. He knows of your wants, your needs, and your fears. The Lord is all powerful. Trust Him.

The Prophet Joseph Smith was taught that "the works, and the designs, and the purposes of God cannot be frustrated, neither can they come to naught" (Doctrine and Covenants 3:1). To His struggling children, the Lord gave these great assurances:

"Behold, this is the promise of the Lord unto you, O ye my servants.

"Wherefore, be of good cheer, and do not fear, for I the Lord am with you, and will stand by you; and ye shall bear record of me, even Jesus Christ, that I am the Son of the living God" (Doctrine and Covenants 68:5–6).

The Lord stands near us, and He has said:

"What I say unto one I say unto all, be of good cheer, little children; for I am in your midst, and I have not forsaken you" (Doctrine and Covenants 61:36).

"For after much tribulation come the blessings" (Doctrine and Covenants 58:4).

Sisters, I testify that these promises, given in the midst of persecutions and personal tragedies, apply to each of you in your troubling circumstances today. They are precious and remind each of us to be of good cheer and to have joy in the fulness of the gospel as we press forward through the challenges of mortality.

Tribulation and challenges are the common experiences of mortality. Opposition is an essential part of the divine plan for helping us grow,[2] and in the midst of that process, we have God's assurance that, in the long view of eternity, opposition will not be allowed to overcome us. With His help and our faithfulness and endurance, we will prevail. Like the mortal life of which they are a part, all tribulations are temporary. In the controversies that preceded a disastrous war, United States president Abraham Lincoln wisely reminded his audience of the ancient wisdom that "this, too, shall pass away."[3]

As you know, the mortal adversities of which I speak—which make it difficult to be of good cheer—sometimes come to us in common with many others, like the millions now struggling through some of the many devastating effects of the COVID-19 pandemic. Similarly, in the United States millions are suffering through a season of enmity and contention that always seems to accompany presidential elections but this time is the most severe many of the oldest of us can ever remember.

On a personal basis, each of us struggles individually with some of the many adversities of mortality, such as poverty, racism, ill health, job losses or disappointments, wayward children, bad marriages or no marriages, and the effects of sin—our own or others'.

Yet, in the midst of all of this, we have that heavenly counsel to be of good cheer and to find joy in the principles and promises of the gospel and the fruits of our labors.[4] That counsel has always been so, for prophets and for all of us. We know this from the experiences of our predecessors and what the Lord said to them.

Remember the circumstances of the Prophet Joseph Smith. Looked at through the lens of adversities, his life was one of poverty, persecution, frustration, family sorrows, and ultimate martyrdom. As he suffered imprisonment, his wife and children and the other Saints suffered incredible hardships as they were driven out of Missouri.

When Joseph pleaded for relief, the Lord answered:

"My son, peace be unto thy soul; thine adversity and thine afflictions shall be but a small moment;

"And then, if thou endure it well, God shall exalt thee on high; thou shalt triumph over all thy foes" (Doctrine and Covenants 121:7–8).

This was the personal, eternal counsel that helped the Prophet Joseph to maintain his native cheery temperament and the love and loyalty of his people. These same qualities strengthened the leaders and pioneers who followed and can strengthen you as well.

Think of those early members! Again and again, they were driven from place to place. Finally they faced the challenges of establishing their homes and the Church in a wilderness.[5] Two years after the initial band of pioneers arrived in the valley of the Great Salt Lake, the pioneers' grip on survival in that hostile area was still precarious. Most members were still on the trail across the plains or struggling to get resources to do so. Yet leaders and members were still of hope and good cheer.

Even though the Saints were not settled in their new homes, at October 1849 general conference a new wave of missionaries was sent out to Scandinavia, France, Germany, Italy, and the South Pacific.[6] At what could have been thought their lowest level, the pioneers rose to new heights. And just three years later, another 98 were also called to begin to gather scattered Israel. One of the Church leaders explained that these missions "are generally, not to be very long ones; probably from 3 to 7 years will be as long as any man will be absent from his family."[7]

Sisters, the First Presidency is concerned about your challenges. We love you and pray for you. At the same time, we often give thanks that our physical challenges—apart from earthquakes, fires, floods, and hurricanes—are usually less than our predecessors faced.

In the midst of hardships, the divine assurance is always "be of good cheer, for I will lead you along. The kingdom is yours and the blessings thereof are yours, and the riches of eternity are yours" (Doctrine and Covenants 78:18). How does this happen? How did it happen for the pioneers? How will it happen to women of God today? By our following prophetic guidance, "the gates of hell shall not prevail against [us]," the Lord said by revelation in April 1830. "Yea," He said, ". . . the Lord God will disperse the powers of darkness from before you, and cause the heavens to shake for your good, and his name's glory" (Doctrine and Covenants 21:6). "Fear not, little flock; do good; let earth and hell combine against you, for if ye are built upon my rock, they cannot prevail" (Doctrine and Covenants 6:34).

With the Lord's promises, we "lift up [our] heart[s] and rejoice" (Doctrine and Covenants 25:13), and "with a glad heart and a cheerful countenance" (Doctrine and Covenants 59:15), we go forward on the covenant path. Most of us do not face decisions of giant proportions, like leaving our homes to pioneer an unknown land. Our decisions are mostly in the daily routines of life, but as the Lord has told us, "Be not weary in well-doing, for ye are laying the foundation of a great work. And out of small things proceedeth that which is great" (Doctrine and Covenants 64:33).

There is boundless power in the doctrine of the restored gospel of Jesus Christ. Our unshakable faith in that doctrine guides our steps and gives us joy. It enlightens our minds and gives strength and confidence to our actions. This guidance and enlightenment and power are promised gifts we have received from our Heavenly Father. By understanding and conforming our lives to that doctrine, including the divine gift of repentance, we can be of good cheer as we keep ourselves on the path toward our eternal destiny—reunion and exaltation with our loving heavenly parents.

"You may be facing overwhelming challenges," Elder Richard G. Scott taught. "Sometimes they are so concentrated, so unrelenting, that you may feel they are beyond your capacity to control. Don't face the world alone. 'Trust in the Lord with all thine heart; and lean not unto thine own understanding' [Proverbs 3:5]. . . . It was intended that life be a challenge, not so that you would fail, but that you might succeed through overcoming."[8]

It is all part of the plan of God the Father and His Son, Jesus Christ, of which I testify, as I pray that we will all persist to our heavenly destination, in the name of Jesus Christ, amen.

Notes

1. See John 13–16.
2. See 2 Nephi 2:11.
3. Abraham Lincoln, address to the Wisconsin State Agricultural Society, Milwaukee, Sept. 30, 1859, in John Bartlett, *Bartlett's Familiar Quotations*, 18th ed. (2012), 444.
4. See Doctrine and Covenants 6:31.
5. See Lawrence E. Corbridge, "Surviving and Thriving like the Pioneers," *Ensign*, July 2020, 23–24.
6. See "Minutes of the General Conference of 6 October 1849," General Church Minutes Collection, Church History Library, Salt Lake City.
7. George A. Smith, in Journal History of The Church of Jesus Christ of Latter-day Saints, Aug. 28, 1852, 1, Church History Library, Salt Lake City.
8. Richard G. Scott, *Finding Peace, Happiness, and Joy* (2007), 248–49.

EMBRACE THE FUTURE WITH FAITH

PRESIDENT RUSSELL M. NELSON
President of The Church of Jesus Christ of Latter-day Saints

My dear sisters, I am honored to be with you. You have been on my mind so often during these past few months. You are more than eight million strong. You have not only the *numbers* but the *spiritual power* to change the world. I have watched you doing just that during this pandemic.

Some of you suddenly found yourselves searching for scarce supplies or a new job. Many tutored children and checked on neighbors. Some welcomed missionaries home earlier than expected, while others transformed your homes into missionary training centers. You have used technology to connect with family and friends, to minister to those who have felt isolated, and to study *Come, Follow Me* with others. You have found new ways to make the Sabbath a delight. And you have made protective masks—millions of them!

With heartfelt compassion and love, my heart goes out to the many women around the world whose loved ones have died. We weep with you. And we pray for you. We praise and pray for all who work tirelessly to safeguard the health of others.

You young women have also been remarkable. Though social media has been flooded with contention, many of you have found ways to encourage others and share our Savior's light.

Sisters, you have all been absolutely heroic! I marvel at your strength and your faith. You have shown that in difficult circumstances, you bravely carry on. I love you, and I assure you that the Lord loves you and sees the great work you are performing. Thank you! Once again, you have proven that you are literally the hope of Israel!

You embody the hopes that President Gordon B. Hinckley had for you when he introduced "The Family: A Proclamation to the World" 25 years ago in the September 1995 general Relief Society meeting.[1] It is significant that he chose to introduce this important proclamation to the sisters of the Church. By doing so, President

Hinckley underscored the irreplaceable influence of women in the Lord's plan.

Now, I would love to know what you have learned this year. Have you grown closer to the Lord, or do you feel further away from Him? And how have current events made you feel about the future?

Admittedly, the Lord has spoken of our day in sobering terms. He warned that in our day "men's hearts [would fail] them"[2] and that even the very elect would be at risk of being deceived.[3] He told the Prophet Joseph Smith that "peace [would] be taken from the earth"[4] and calamities would befall mankind.[5]

Yet the Lord has also provided a vision of how remarkable this dispensation is. He inspired the Prophet Joseph Smith to declare that "the work of . . . these last days, is one of vast magnitude. . . . Its glories are past description, and its grandeur unsurpassable."[6]

Now, *grandeur* may not be the word you would choose to describe these past few months! How *are* we to deal with both the somber prophecies and the glorious pronouncements about our day? The Lord told us how with simple, but stunning, reassurance: "If ye are prepared ye shall not fear."[7]

What a promise! It is one that can literally change the way we see our future. I recently heard a woman of deep testimony admit that the pandemic, combined with an earthquake in the Salt Lake Valley, had helped her realize she was not as prepared as she thought she was. When I asked whether she was referring to her food storage *or* her testimony, she smiled and said, "Yes!"

If preparation is our key to embracing this dispensation and our future with faith, how can we best prepare?

For decades, the Lord's prophets have urged us to store food, water, and financial reserves for a time of need. The current pandemic has reinforced the wisdom of that counsel. I urge you to take steps to be temporally prepared. But I am even more concerned about your spiritual and emotional preparation.

In that regard, we can learn a lot from Captain Moroni. As commander of the Nephite armies, he faced opposing forces that were stronger, greater in number, and meaner. So, Moroni prepared his people in three essential ways.

First, he helped them create areas where they would be safe—"places of security" he called them.[8] **Second,** he prepared "the minds of the people to be faithful unto the Lord."[9] And **third,** he never stopped preparing his people—physically or spiritually.[10] Let us consider these three principles.

Principle Number One: Create Places of Security

Moroni fortified every Nephite city with embankments, forts, and walls.[11] When the Lamanites came against them, they "were astonished exceedingly, because of the wisdom of the Nephites in preparing *their places of security.*"[12]

Similarly, as turmoil rages around *us,* we need to create places where *we* are safe, both physically and spiritually. When your home becomes a personal sanctuary of faith—where the Spirit resides—your home becomes the first line of defense.

Likewise, the stakes of Zion are "a refuge from the storm"[13] because they are led by those who hold priesthood keys and exercise priesthood authority. As you continue to follow the counsel of those whom the Lord has authorized to guide you, you will feel greater safety.

The temple—the house of the Lord—is a place of security unlike any other. There, you sisters are endowed with priesthood power through the sacred priesthood covenants you make.[14] There, your families are sealed for eternity. Even this year, when access to our temples has been seriously limited, your endowment has given you constant access to God's power as you have honored your covenants with Him.

Simply said, a place of security is *anywhere* you can feel the presence of the Holy Ghost and be guided by Him.[15] When the Holy Ghost is with you, you can teach truth, even when it runs counter to prevailing opinions. And you can ponder sincere questions about the gospel in an environment of revelation.

I invite you, my dear sisters, to create a home that is a place of security. And I renew my invitation for you to increase your understanding of priesthood power and of temple covenants and blessings. Having places of security to which you can retreat will help you embrace the future with faith.

Principle Number Two: Prepare Your Mind to Be Faithful to God

We have undertaken a major project to extend the life and capacity of the Salt Lake Temple.

Some questioned the need for taking such extraordinary measures. However, when the Salt Lake Valley suffered a 5.7-magnitude earthquake earlier this year, this venerable temple shook hard enough that the trumpet on the statue of the angel Moroni fell![16]

Just as the physical foundation of the Salt Lake Temple must be strong enough to withstand natural disasters, our *spiritual* foundations must be solid. Then, when metaphorical earthquakes rock our lives, we can stand "steadfast and immovable" because of our faith.[17]

The Lord taught us how to increase our faith by seeking "*learning,* even by study and also by faith."[18] We strengthen our faith in Jesus Christ as we strive to keep His commandments and "always remember him."[19] Further, our faith increases every time we *exercise* our faith in Him. That is what learning by faith means.

For example, each time we have the faith to be obedient to God's laws—even when popular opinions belittle us—or each time we resist entertainment or ideologies that celebrate covenant-breaking, we are *exercising* our faith, which in turn *increases* our faith.

Further, few things build faith more than does regular immersion in the Book of Mormon. No other book testifies of Jesus Christ with such power and clarity. Its prophets, as inspired by the Lord, saw our day and selected the doctrine and truths that would help *us* most. The Book of Mormon *is* our *latter-day* survival guide.

Of course, our ultimate security comes as we yoke ourselves to Heavenly Father and Jesus Christ! Life *without* God is a life filled with fear. Life *with* God is a life filled with peace. This is because spiritual blessings come to the faithful. Receiving personal revelation is one of the greatest of those blessings.

The Lord has promised that if we will ask, we may receive "revelation upon revelation."[20] I promise that as you increase your capacity to receive revelation, the Lord will bless you with increased direction for your life and with boundless gifts of the Spirit.

Principle Number Three: Never Stop Preparing

Even when things went *well,* Captain Moroni continued to prepare his people. He never stopped. He *never* became complacent.

The adversary never stops attacking. So, we can *never* stop preparing! The more self-reliant we are—temporally, emotionally, and spiritually—the more prepared we are to thwart Satan's relentless assaults.

Dear sisters, you are adept at creating places of security for yourselves and those you love. Further, you have a divine endowment that enables you to build faith in others in compelling ways.[21] And *you* never stop. You have demonstrated that once again this year.

Please, keep going! Your vigilance in safeguarding your homes and instilling faith in the hearts of your loved ones will reap rewards for generations to come.

My dear sisters, we have *so much* to look forward to! The Lord placed you here now because He knew you had the capacity to negotiate the complexities of the latter part of these latter days. He knew you would grasp the grandeur of His work and be eager to help bring it to pass.

I am not saying that the days ahead will be easy, but I promise you that the future will be glorious for those who are prepared and who continue to prepare to be instruments in the Lord's hands.

My dear sisters, let us not just *endure* this current season. Let us *embrace the future with faith*! Turbulent times are opportunities for us to thrive spiritually. They are times when our influence can be much more penetrating than in calmer times.

I promise that as we create places of security, prepare our minds to be faithful to God, and never stop preparing, God will bless us.

He will "deliver us; yea, insomuch that he [will] speak peace to our souls, and [will] grant unto us great faith, and . . . cause us that we [can] hope for our deliverance in him."[22]

As you prepare to embrace the future with faith, these promises *will* be yours! I so testify, with my expression of love *for* you and my confidence *in* you, in the sacred name of Jesus Christ, amen.

Notes

1. See "The Family: A Proclamation to the World," ChurchofJesusChrist.org. In the address that accompanied this proclamation, President Gordon B. Hinckley said to the sisters: "I am grateful for the strength that you have and for your loyalty, your faith, your love. I am thankful for the resolution which you carry in your hearts to walk in faith, to keep the commandments, to do what is right at all times and in all circumstances" ("Stand Strong against the Wiles of the World," *Ensign*, Nov. 1995, 98–99).
2. Luke 21:26; see also Doctrine and Covenants 45:26.
3. See Matthew 24:24; Joseph Smith—Matthew 1:22.
4. Doctrine and Covenants 1:35.
5. See Doctrine and Covenants 1:17. The Apostle Paul prophesied that "in the last days perilous times [would] come." That would make our day spiritually treacherous. (See 2 Timothy 3:1–5.)
6. *Teachings of Presidents of the Church: Joseph Smith* (2007), 512.
7. Doctrine and Covenants 38:30.
8. See Alma 49:5; 50:4.
9. Alma 48:7.
10. See Alma 49–50.
11. See Alma 48:8.
12. Alma 49:5; emphasis added.
13. Doctrine and Covenants 115:6.
14. See Russell M. Nelson, "Spiritual Treasures," *Ensign* or *Liahona*, Nov. 2019, 76–79.
15. Eliza R. Snow taught that the Holy Ghost "satisfies and fills up every longing of the human heart. . . . When I am filled with that Spirit, my soul is satisfied, and I can say in good earnest, that the trifling things of the day do not seem to stand in my way at all. . . . Is it not our privilege to so live that we can have this constantly flowing into our souls?" (in *Daughters in My Kingdom: The History and Work of Relief Society* [2011], 46).
16. See Daniel Burke, "Utah Earthquake Damages Mormon Temple and Knocks Trumpet from Iconic Angel Statue," Mar. 18, 2020, cnn.com.
17. Mosiah 5:15.
18. Doctrine and Covenants 88:118; emphasis added.
19. Moroni 4:3.
20. Doctrine and Covenants 42:61.
21. The Apostle Paul signaled this reality when he attributed Timothy's unfeigned faith to his mother, Eunice, and his grandmother Lois (see 2 Timothy 1:5).
22. Alma 58:11.

SUNDAY MORNING SESSION

OCTOBER 4, 2020

WATCH YE THEREFORE, AND PRAY ALWAYS

PRESIDENT M. RUSSELL BALLARD
Acting President of the Quorum of the Twelve Apostles

My dear brothers and sisters, during the last week of His mortal ministry, Jesus taught His disciples to "*watch ye therefore, and pray always,* that ye may be accounted worthy to escape all these things that shall come to pass, and to stand before the Son of man."[1]

Among the "things that shall come to pass" before His Second Coming are "wars and rumours of wars[,] . . . famines, and pestilences, and earthquakes, in divers places."[2]

In the Doctrine and Covenants, the Savior said, *"And all things shall be in commotion; . . . for fear shall come upon all people."*[3]

Certainly, we live in a time during which things are in commotion. Many people fear the future, and many hearts have turned away from their faith in God and His Son, Jesus Christ.

News reports are filled with accounts of violence. Moral denigration is published online. Cemeteries, churches, mosques, synagogues, and religious shrines have been vandalized.

A global pandemic has reached virtually every corner of the earth: millions of people have been infected; over a million have died. School graduations, church worship services, marriages, missionary service, and a host of other important life events have been disrupted. Additionally, countless people have been left alone and isolated.

Economic upheavals have caused challenges for so many, especially for the most vulnerable of our Heavenly Father's children.

We have seen people passionately exercising their right to peaceful protest, and we have seen angry mobs riot.

At the same time, we continue to see conflicts all around the world.

I think often of those of you who are suffering, worried, afraid, or feeling alone. I assure each one of you that the Lord knows you, that He is aware of your concern and anguish, and that He loves you—intimately, personally, deeply, and forever.

Each night when I pray, I ask the Lord to bless all who are burdened with grief, pain, loneliness, and sadness. I know that other Church leaders echo that same prayer. Our hearts, individually and collectively, go out to you, and our prayers go to God in your behalf.

I spent several days last year in the northeastern part of the United States visiting American and Church history sites, attending meetings with our missionaries and our members, and visiting government and business leaders.

On Sunday, October 20, I spoke to a large gathering near Boston, Massachusetts. As I was speaking, I was prompted to say, "I plead with you . . . to pray for this country, for our leaders, for our people, and for the families that live in this great nation founded by God."[4]

I also said that America and many of the nations of the earth, as in times past, are at another critical crossroads and need our prayers.[5]

My plea was not in my prepared remarks. Those words came to me as I felt the Spirit prompt me to invite those present to pray for their country and their leaders.

Today I expand my call for prayer to all people from every country around the world. No matter how you pray or to whom you pray, please exercise your faith—whatever your faith may be—and pray for your country and for your national leaders. As I said last October in Massachusetts, we stand today at a major crossroads in history, and the nations of the earth are in desperate need of divine inspiration and guidance. This is not about politics or policy. This is about peace and the healing that can come to individual souls as well as to the soul of countries—their cities, towns, and villages—through the Prince of Peace and the source of all healing, the Lord Jesus Christ.

During the past few months I have had the impression come to me that the best way to help the current world situation is for all people to rely more fully upon God and to turn their hearts to Him through sincere prayer. Humbling ourselves and seeking heaven's inspiration to endure or conquer what is before us will be our safest and surest way to move confidently forward through these troubling times.

The scriptures highlight prayers offered by Jesus as well as His teachings about prayer during His mortal ministry. You will remember the Lord's Prayer:

"Our Father which art in heaven, Hallowed be thy name.

"Thy kingdom come. Thy will be done in earth, as it is in heaven.

"Give us this day our daily bread.

"And forgive us our debts, as we forgive our debtors.

"And lead us not into temptation, but deliver us from evil: For thine is the kingdom, and the power, and the glory, for ever. Amen."[6]

This focused, beautiful prayer, repeated often throughout Christianity, makes it clear that it is appropriate to directly petition "our Father which art in heaven" for answers to what is troubling us. Therefore, let us pray for divine guidance.

I invite you to pray always.[7] Pray for your family. Pray for the leaders of nations. Pray for the courageous people who are on the front lines in the current battles against social, environmental, political, and biological plagues that impact all people throughout the world: the rich and the poor, the young and the old.

The Savior taught us to not limit who we pray for. He said, "Love your enemies, bless them that curse you, do good to them that hate you, and pray for them which despitefully use you, and persecute you."[8]

On the cross of Calvary, where Jesus died for our sins, He practiced what He taught when He prayed, "Father, forgive them; for they know not what they do."[9]

Sincerely praying for those who may be considered our enemies demonstrates our belief that God can change our hearts and the hearts of others. Such prayers should strengthen our resolve to make whatever changes are necessary in our own lives, families, and communities.

No matter where you live, what language you speak, or the challenges you face, God hears and answers you in His own way and in His own time. Because we are His children, we can approach Him to seek help, solace, and a renewed desire to make a positive difference in the world.

Praying for justice, peace, the poor, and the sick is often not enough. After we *kneel* in prayer, we need to get up from our knees and do what we can to help—to help both ourselves and others.[10]

The scriptures are full of examples of people of faith who combined prayer with action to make a difference in their own lives and in the lives of others. In the Book of Mormon, for example, we read about Enos. It has been observed that "about two-thirds of his short book describes a prayer or series of prayers, and the balance tells what he did in consequence of the answers he received."[11]

We have many examples of how prayer made a difference in our own Church history, beginning with Joseph Smith's first vocal prayer in a wooded clearing near his parents' log home in the spring of 1820. Seeking forgiveness and spiritual direction, Joseph's prayer opened the heavens. Today we are the beneficiaries of Joseph the Prophet and other faithful Latter-day Saint men and women who prayed and acted to help establish The Church of Jesus Christ of Latter-day Saints.

I often think of the prayers of faithful women like Mary Fielding Smith who, with God's help, courageously led her family from mounting persecution in Illinois to safety in this valley, where her family prospered spiritually and temporally. After praying earnestly on her knees, she then worked hard to overcome her challenges and bless her family.

Prayer will lift us and draw us together as individuals, as families, as a church, and as a world. Prayer will influence scientists and help them toward discoveries of vaccines and medications that will end this pandemic. Prayer will comfort those who have lost a loved one. It will guide us in knowing what to do for our own personal protection.

Brothers and sisters, I urge you to redouble your commitment to prayer. I urge you to pray in your closets, in your daily walk, in your homes, in your wards, and always in your hearts.[12]

On behalf of the leaders of The Church of Jesus Christ of Latter-day Saints, I thank you for your prayers for us. I urge you to continue to pray that we may receive the inspiration and revelation to guide the Church through these difficult times.

Prayer can change our own lives. Motivated by sincere prayer, we can improve and help others to do the same.

I know the power of prayer by my own experience. Recently I was alone in my office. I had just gone through a medical procedure on my hand. It was black and blue, swollen, and it was painful. As I sat at my desk, I could not focus on important and critical matters because I was distracted by this pain.

I knelt in prayer and asked the Lord to help me focus so I could accomplish my work. I stood and returned to the pile of papers on my desk. Almost immediately, clarity and focus came to my mind, and I was able to complete the pressing matters before me.

The world's current chaotic situation may seem daunting as we consider the multitude of issues and challenges. But it is my fervent testimony that if we will pray and ask Heavenly Father for needed blessings and guidance, we will come to know how we can bless our families, neighbors, communities, and even the countries in which we live.

The Savior prayed and then He "went about doing good"[13] by feeding the poor, providing courage and support to those in need, and reaching out in love, forgiveness, peace, and rest to all who would come unto Him. He continues to reach out to us.

I invite all Church members, as well as our neighbors and friends of other faith groups worldwide, to do as the Savior counseled His disciples: "*Watch ye therefore, and pray always*"[14] for peace, for comfort, for safety, and for opportunities to serve one another.

How great is the power of prayer, and how needed are our prayers of faith in God and His Beloved Son in the world today! Let us remember and appreciate the power of prayer. In the name of Jesus Christ, amen.

Notes

1. Luke 21:36; emphasis added.
2. Matthew 24:6, 7.
3. Doctrine and Covenants 88:91; emphasis added.
4. M. Russell Ballard, in Sarah Jane Weaver, "President Ballard Pleads with Latter-day Saints to

'Pray for This Country' as United States Is at 'Another Crossroad,'" *Church News*, Oct. 21, 2019, thechurchnews.com.

5. See Weaver, "President Ballard Pleads with Latter-day Saints."
6. Matthew 6:9–13. Notice that the Joseph Smith Translation clarifies verse 13: "And suffer [permit] us not to be led into temptation, but deliver us from evil" (Joseph Smith Translation, Matthew 6:14 [in Matthew 6:13, footnote a]).
7. See Luke 18:1–8; 21:36; Ephesians 6:18; 2 Nephi 32:9; 3 Nephi 18:15, 18–21; Doctrine and Covenants 10:5; 19:38; 33:17; 61:39; 88:126; 90:24.
8. Matthew 5:44.
9. Luke 23:34.
10. See Alma 34:27–29.
11. Sharon J. Harris, *Enos, Jarom, Omni: A Brief Theological Introduction* (2020), 18.
12. See Alma 33:3–11; 34:17–27.
13. Acts 10:38.
14. Luke 21:36, emphasis added; see also 3 Nephi 18:15.

PEACE, BE STILL

LISA L. HARKNESS

First Counselor in the Primary General Presidency

When our children were young, our family spent a few days at a beautiful lake. One afternoon some of the children put on life jackets before jumping off a deck and into the water. Our youngest daughter watched with hesitation, carefully observing her siblings. With all the courage she could muster, she plugged her nose with one hand and jumped. She immediately popped up and with a bit of panic in her voice yelled, "Help me! Help me!"

Now, she was not in any mortal danger; her life jacket was doing its job, and she was floating safely. We could have reached out and pulled her back on the deck with little effort. Yet from her perspective, she needed help. Perhaps it was the chill of the water or the newness of the experience. In any case, she climbed back onto the deck, where we wrapped her in a dry towel and complimented her on her bravery.

Whether we are old or young, many of us have, in moments of distress, uttered with urgency words such as "Help me!" "Save me!" or "Please, answer my prayer!"

Such an event happened with Jesus's disciples during His mortal ministry. In Mark we read that Jesus "began again to teach by the sea side: and there was gathered unto him a great multitude."[1] The crowd became so numerous that Jesus "entered into a ship"[2] and spoke from its deck. All day long He taught the people in parables as they sat on the shore.

"And . . . when the [evening] was come," He said unto His disciples, "Let us pass over unto the other side. And when they had sent away the multitude,"[3] they departed from the shore and were on their way across the Sea of Galilee. Finding a spot in the back of the ship, Jesus lay down and quickly fell asleep. Soon "there arose a great storm of wind, and the waves beat into the ship, so that it was [nearly] full"[4] of water.

Many of Jesus's disciples were experienced fishermen and knew how to handle a boat in a storm. They were His trusted—indeed, His beloved—disciples. They had left jobs, personal interests, and family to follow Jesus. Their faith in Him was evident by their presence in the boat. And now their boat was in the middle of a tempest and on the very verge of sinking.

We don't know how long they battled to keep the boat afloat in the storm, but they woke Jesus with a bit of panic in their voices, saying:

"Master, carest thou not that we perish?"[5]

"Lord, save us: we perish."[6]

They called Him "Master," and that He is. He is also "Jesus Christ, the Son of God, the Father of heaven and earth, the Creator of all things from the beginning."[7]

From His position in the boat, Jesus arose and rebuked the wind and said unto the raging sea, "Peace, be still. And the wind [did cease], and there was a great calm."[8] Ever the Master Teacher, Jesus then taught His disciples through two simple yet loving questions. He asked:

"Why are ye so fearful?"[9]

"Where is your faith?"[10]

There is a mortal tendency, even a temptation, when we find ourselves in the middle of trials, troubles, or afflictions to cry out, "Master, carest thou not that I perish? Save me." Even Joseph Smith pleaded from an awful prison, "O God, where art thou? And where is the pavilion that covereth thy hiding place?"[11]

Certainly, the Savior of the world understands our mortal limitations, for He teaches us how to feel peace and calm even when the winds blow fiercely around us and billowing waves threaten to sink our hopes.

To those with proven faith, childlike faith, or even the smallest particle of faith,[12] Jesus invites, saying: "Come unto me."[13] "Believe on my name."[14] "Learn of me, and listen to my words."[15] He tenderly commands, "Repent and [be] baptized in my name,"[16] "Love one another; as I have loved you,"[17] and "Always remember me."[18] Jesus reassures, explaining: "These things I have spoken unto you, that in me ye might have peace. In the world ye shall have tribulation: but be of good cheer; I have overcome the world."[19]

I can imagine that Jesus's disciples in the storm-tossed boat were, of necessity, busy watching the waves crash onto their deck and bailing out the water. I can picture them handling the sails and trying to maintain some semblance of control over their little craft. Their focus was on surviving the moment, and their plea for help was urgently sincere.

Many of us are no different in our day. Recent events around the globe and in our nations, communities, and families have buffeted us with unforeseen trials. In times of turmoil our faith can feel stretched to the limits of our endurance and understanding. Waves of fear can distract us, causing us to forget God's goodness, thus leaving our perspective short-sighted and out of focus. Yet it is in these rough stretches of our journey that our faith can be not only tried but fortified.

Regardless of our circumstances, we can intentionally make efforts to build and increase our faith in Jesus Christ. It is strengthened when we remember that we are children of God and that He loves us. Our faith grows as we experiment on the word of God with hope and diligence, trying our very best to follow Christ's teachings. Our faith increases as we choose to believe rather than doubt, forgive rather than judge, repent rather than rebel. Our faith is refined as we patiently rely on the merits and mercy and grace of the Holy Messiah.[20]

"While faith is not a perfect knowledge," Elder Neal A. Maxwell said, "it brings a deep trust in God, whose knowledge is perfect!"[21] Even in turbulent times, faith in the Lord Jesus Christ is gritty and resilient. It helps us sift through unimportant distractions. It encourages us to keep moving along the covenant path. Faith pushes through discouragement and allows us to face the future with resolve and squared shoulders. It prompts us to ask for rescue and relief as we pray to the Father in the name of His Son. And when prayerful pleas seem to go unanswered, our persistent faith in Jesus Christ produces patience, humility, and the ability to reverently utter the words "Thy will be done."[22]

President Russell M. Nelson has taught:

"We do not need to let our fears displace our faith. We can combat those fears by strengthening our faith.

"Start with your children. . . . Let them feel your faith, even when sore trials come upon you. Let your faith be focused on our loving Heavenly Father and His Beloved Son, the Lord Jesus Christ. . . . Teach each precious boy or girl that he or she is a child of God, created in His image, with a sacred purpose and potential. Each is born with challenges to overcome and faith to be developed."[23]

I recently heard two four-year-old children share their faith in Jesus Christ when they responded to the question "How does Jesus Christ help you?" The first child said, "I know Jesus loves me because He died for me. He also loves grown-ups." The second child said, "He helps me when I'm sad or grumpy. He also helps me when I'm sinking."

Jesus declared, "Therefore, whoso repenteth and cometh unto me as a little child, him will I receive, for of such is the kingdom of God."[24]

"For God so loved the world, that he gave his only begotten Son, that whosoever believeth in him should not perish, but have everlasting life."[25]

Recently, President Nelson promised "that decreased fear and increased faith will follow" as we "begin anew *truly* to hear, hearken to, and heed the words of the Savior."[26]

Sisters and brothers, our current challenging circumstances are not our final, eternal destination. As members of The Church of Jesus Christ of Latter-day Saints, we have taken upon us the name of Jesus Christ by covenant. We have faith in His redeeming power and hope in His great and precious promises. We have every reason to rejoice, for our Lord and Savior is keenly aware of our troubles, cares, and sorrows. As Jesus was with His disciples of old, He is in our boat! I testify He has given His life so that you and I will not perish. May we trust Him, obey His commandments, and with faith hear Him say, "Peace, be still."[27] In the sacred and holy name of Jesus Christ, amen.

Notes

1. Mark 4:1.
2. Mark 4:1.
3. Mark 4:35–36.
4. Mark 4:37.
5. Mark 4:38.
6. Matthew 8:25.
7. Mosiah 3:8.
8. Mark 4:39.
9. Mark 4:40.
10. Luke 8:25.
11. Doctrine and Covenants 121:1.
12. See Alma 32:27.
13. Matthew 11:28.
14. Ether 3:14.
15. Doctrine and Covenants 19:23.
16. 3 Nephi 18:11.
17. John 13:34.
18. 3 Nephi 18:7.
19. John 16:33.
20. See 2 Nephi 2:8.
21. Neal A. Maxwell, "Lest Ye Be Wearied and Faint in Your Minds," *Ensign*, May 1991, 89.
22. Luke 11:2.
23. Russell M. Nelson, "Face the Future with Faith," *Ensign* or *Liahona*, May 2011, 34.
24. 3 Nephi 9:22.
25. John 3:16.
26. Russell M. Nelson, "Go Forward in Faith," *Ensign* or *Liahona*, May 2020, 114.
27. Mark 4:39.

SEEK CHRIST IN EVERY THOUGHT

ELDER ULISSES SOARES

Of the Quorum of the Twelve Apostles

In his poetic hymn of praise, the Psalmist declared:

"O Lord, thou hast searched me, and known me.

"Thou knowest my downsitting and mine uprising, thou understandest my thought afar off.

"Thou compassest my path and my lying down, and art acquainted with all my ways."[1]

In this poem's semantic parallelism, the Psalmist praises the Lord's divine attribute of omniscience because He truly knows every aspect of our souls.[2] Being aware of all that is necessary for us in this life, the Savior invites us to seek Him in every thought and to follow Him with all our heart.[3] This gives us the promise that we can walk in His light and that His guidance prevents the influence of darkness in our life.[4]

Seeking Christ in every thought and following Him with all our heart requires that we align our mind and desires with His.[5] The scriptures refer to this alignment as "stand[ing] fast in the Lord."[6] This course of action implies that we continually conduct our lives in harmony with the gospel of Christ and focus daily on everything that is good.[7] Only then may we achieve "the peace of God, which passeth all understanding" and which will "keep [our] hearts and minds through Christ Jesus."[8] The Savior Himself instructed the elders of the Church in February 1831, "Treasure these things up in your hearts, and let the solemnities of eternity rest upon your minds."[9]

Despite our continuous efforts to seek out the Lord, inappropriate thoughts may penetrate our mind. When such thoughts are permitted and even invited to stay, they can shape the desires of our heart and lead us to what we will become in this life and eventually to what we will inherit for eternity.[10] Elder Neal A. Maxwell once emphasized this principle by saying, "Desires . . . determine the gradations in outcomes, including why 'many are called, but few are chosen.'"[11]

Our ancient and modern prophets have constantly reminded us to resist temptation in order to avoid losing our spiritual traction and becoming confused, disoriented, and disillusioned in life.

Metaphorically speaking, yielding to temptation is like approaching a magnet with a metal object. The magnet's invisible force attracts the metal object and holds it tightly. The magnet loses its power over it only when the metal object is placed far from it. Therefore, just as the magnet is unable to exercise power over a faraway metal object, as we resist temptation, it fades away and loses its power over our mind and heart and, consequently, over our actions.

This analogy reminds me of an experience that a very faithful member of the Church shared with me some time ago. This member told me that when she awakened on one particular morning, an improper thought that she had never experienced before unexpectedly entered her mind. Although it caught her completely by surprise, she reacted against the situation in a split second, saying to herself and to that thought, "No!" and replaced it with something good to divert her mind from the unwelcome thought. She told me that as she exercised her moral agency in righteousness, that negative, involuntary thought immediately disappeared.

When Moroni called upon the people to believe in Christ and to repent, he urged them to come unto the Savior with all their hearts, stripping themselves from all uncleanness. Furthermore, Moroni invited them to ask God, with unbreakable determination, that they would not fall into temptation.[12] Applying these principles in our lives requires more than a mere belief; it requires adjusting our minds and hearts to these divine principles. Such adjustment requires a daily and constant personal effort, in addition to reliance on the Savior, because our mortal inclinations will not disappear on their own. Fighting against temptation takes a lifetime of diligence and faithfulness. But please know that the Lord is ready to assist us in our personal efforts and promises remarkable blessings if we endure to the end.

During a particularly difficult time when Joseph Smith and his fellow prisoners in Liberty Jail did not have freedom in anything except for their thoughts, the Lord provided helpful counsel and a promise to them that are extended to all of us:

"Let thy bowels also be full of charity towards all men [and women], and to the household of faith, and let virtue garnish thy thoughts unceasingly; then shall thy confidence wax strong in the presence of God; . . .

"The Holy Ghost shall be thy constant companion, and thy scepter an unchanging scepter of righteousness and truth."[13]

In doing so, holy thoughts will continuously adorn our minds and pure desires will lead us to righteous actions.

Moroni also reminded his people not to be consumed by their lusts.[14] The word *lust* refers to an intense longing and improper desire for something.[15] It encompasses any dark thoughts or evil desires that cause an individual to focus on selfish practices or worldly possessions rather than doing good, being kind, keeping the commandments of God, and so forth. It is often manifested through the most carnal feelings of the soul. The Apostle Paul identified some of these feelings, such as "uncleanness, lasciviousness, . . . hatred, . . . wrath, strife, . . . envyings, . . . and such like."[16] Besides all the evil aspects of lust, we cannot forget that the enemy uses it as a secret and deceptive weapon against us when he tempts us to do something wrong.

My beloved brothers and sisters, I testify that as we rely upon the rock of salvation, the Savior of our souls, and follow Moroni's counsel, our ability to control our thoughts will increase significantly. I can assure you that our spiritual maturity will grow at an increasing pace, changing our heart, making us more like Jesus Christ. Additionally, the influence of the Holy Ghost will be more intense and continuous in our life. Then the enemy's temptations, little by little, will lose their power over us, resulting in a happier and more pure and consecrated life.

For those who, for whatever reason, fall into temptation and are dwelling upon unrighteous actions, I assure you that there is a way back, that there is hope in Christ. A few years ago, I had the opportunity to visit with a dear member of The Church of Jesus Christ of Latter-day Saints who went through a very difficult time in his life after committing a major transgression. When I first saw him, I could see a sadness in his eyes, accompanied by a brightness of hope in his countenance. His very expression reflected a humble and changed heart. He had been a dedicated Christian and had been richly blessed by the Lord. However, he had let a single improper thought invade his mind, which then led to others. As he steadily became more and more permissive of these thoughts, soon they took root in his mind and began to grow deep in his heart. He eventually acted upon these unworthy desires, which led him to make decisions against everything that was most precious in his life. He told me that if he had not given place to that foolish thought to begin with, he would not have become vulnerable and susceptible to the temptations of the enemy—temptations that brought so much sadness in his life, at least for a period of time.

Fortunately, like the prodigal son in the famous parable found in the Gospel of Luke, "he came to himself" and woke up from that nightmare.[17] He renewed his trust in the Lord and felt true contrition and had the desire to eventually return to the Lord's fold. That day we both felt the Savior's redeeming love for us. At the end of our brief visit, we were both overcome with emotion, and to this day, I remember the resplendent joy in his countenance when he left my office.

My dear friends, when we resist the little temptations, which often come unexpectedly in our life, we are better equipped to avoid serious transgressions. As President Spencer W. Kimball said: "Seldom does one enter into deeper transgression without first yielding to lesser ones, which open the door to the greater. . . . 'A clean field [does not] suddenly [become] weedy.'"[18]

While preparing to accomplish His divine mission on earth, the Savior Jesus Christ exemplified the importance of constantly resisting everything that might dissuade us from realizing our eternal purpose. After several unsuccessful attacks by the enemy, who attempted to divert Him from His mission, the Savior categorically dismissed the devil by saying: "Get thee hence, Satan. . . . Then the devil leaveth him, and, behold, angels came and ministered unto him."[19]

Can you imagine, my brothers and sisters, what would happen if we were to derive strength and courage from the Savior and say, "No" and "Get thee hence" to unvirtuous thoughts that very first moment they come into our minds? What would be the impact on the desires of our hearts? How would our resulting actions keep us close to the Savior and allow the continued influence of the Holy Ghost in our lives? I know that by following Jesus's example, we will avoid many tragedies and undesirable behaviors that might cause family problems and disagreements, negative emotions and inclinations, perpetrating injustices and abuses, enslavement by evil addictions, and anything else that would be against the Lord's commandments.

In his historic and touching message from April this year, our dear prophet, President Russell M. Nelson, made a promise that all those who are willing to "hear Him"—hear Jesus Christ—and obey His commandments "will be blessed with additional power to deal with temptation, struggles, and weakness" and that our capacity to feel joy will increase, even during the increasing current turbulence.[20]

I testify to you that the promises given by our dear prophet are the promises given by the Savior Himself. I invite all of us to "hear Him" in every thought and follow Him with all our heart in order to obtain the strength and courage to say, "No" and "Get thee hence" to all the things that might bring unhappiness into our life. If we do so, I promise that the Lord will send an added measure of His Holy Spirit to strengthen and comfort us and we may become individuals after the Lord's own heart.[21]

I bear my witness that Jesus Christ lives and that through Him, we may triumph over the enemy's evil influences and qualify to live for eternity with the Lord and in the presence of our beloved Father in Heaven. I testify of these truths with all my love for you and for our beautiful Savior, to whose name I give glory, honor, and praise evermore. I say these things in the sacred name of Jesus Christ, amen.

Notes

1. Psalm 139:1–3.
2. See Guide to the Scriptures, "Omniscient," scriptures.ChurchofJesusChrist.org; see also Matthew 6:8; 2 Nephi 2:24; 3 Nephi 28:6; Doctrine and Covenants 6:16.
3. See Psalm 119:2; Isaiah 45:22; Mosiah 7:33; Doctrine and Covenants 6:36.
4. See John 8:12.
5. See Doctrine and Covenants 68:4.
6. Philippians 4:1.
7. See Philippians 4:8.
8. Philippians 4:7.
9. Doctrine and Covenants 43:34.
10. See Proverbs 23:7; Jeremiah 17:10; 2 Nephi 9:39; Mosiah 4:30; Alma 12:14; Doctrine and Covenants 137:9.
11. Neal A. Maxwell, "According to the Desire of [Our] Hearts," *Ensign*, Nov. 1996, 22; see also Matthew 22:14; Doctrine and Covenants 95:5.
12. See Mormon 9:27–29; see also Mosiah 2:41.
13. Doctrine and Covenants 121:45–46.
14. See Mormon 9:28.
15. See Guide to the Scriptures, "Lust," scriptures.ChurchofJesusChrist.org.
16. Galatians 5:19–21.
17. Luke 15:17.
18. *Teachings of Presidents of the Church: Spencer W. Kimball* (2006), 106; see also 2 Samuel 11.
19. Matthew 4:10–11.
20. Russell M. Nelson, "Hear Him," *Ensign* or *Liahona*, May 2020, 90.
21. See 1 Samuel 13:14.

I BELIEVE IN ANGELS

ELDER CARLOS A. GODOY

Of the Presidency of the Seventy

Brothers and sisters, I believe in angels, and I would like to share with you my experiences with them. In doing so, I hope and pray that we will recognize the importance of angels in our lives.

Here are Elder Jeffrey R. Holland's words from a past general conference: "When we speak of those who are instruments in the hand of God, we are reminded that not all angels are from the other side of the veil. Some of them we walk with and talk with—here, now, every day. Some of them reside in our own neighborhoods. . . . Indeed heaven never seems closer than when we see the love of God manifested in the kindness and devotion of people so good and so pure that *angelic* is the only word that comes to mind" ("The Ministry of Angels," *Ensign* or *Liahona,* Nov. 2008, 30).

It is about angels on this side of the veil that I want to talk. The angels that walk among us in our everyday lives are powerful reminders of God's love for us.

The first angels that I will mention are the two sister missionaries who taught me the gospel when I was a young man: Sister Vilma Molina and Sister Ivonete Rivitti. My younger sister and I were invited to a Church activity where we met these two angels. I never imagined how much that simple activity would change my life.

My parents and siblings were not interested in learning more about the Church at that time. They were not even willing to have the missionaries in our home, so I took the missionary lessons in a Church building. That small room in the chapel became my "sacred grove."

One month after these angels introduced me to the gospel, I was baptized. I was 16 years old.

As you can imagine, remaining active in the Church was challenging for a teenager whose lifestyle had just changed and whose family was not taking the same path.

As I was trying to adjust to my new life, a new culture, and new friends, I felt out of place. I felt alone and discouraged many times. I knew the Church was true, but I had a hard time feeling part of it. While uncomfortable and uncertain as I tried to fit into my new religion, I found the courage to participate in a three-day youth conference, which I thought would help me make new friends. This is when I met another saving angel, named Mônica Brandão.

She was new in the area, having moved from another part of Brazil. She quickly got my attention and, luckily for me, accepted me as a friend. I guess she looked at me more from the inside than the outside.

Because she befriended me, I was introduced to her friends, who then became my friends as we enjoyed many youth activities I attended later. Those activities were so critical to my integration into this new life.

These good friends made a big difference, but not having the gospel taught in my home with a supportive family still put my ongoing conversion process at risk. My gospel interactions in the Church became even more crucial to my growing conversion. Then two additional angels were sent by the Lord to help.

One of them was Leda Vettori, my early-morning seminary teacher. Through her accepting love and inspiring classes, she gave me a daily dose of the "good word of God" (Moroni 6:4), which was so needed throughout my day. This helped me to gain the spiritual strength to keep going.

Another angel sent to help me was the Young Men president, Marco Antônio Fusco. He was also assigned to be my senior home teaching companion. Despite my lack of experience and different appearance, he gave me assignments to teach in our priests quorum meetings and home teaching visits. He gave me the chance to act and to learn and not just be an observer of the gospel. He trusted me, more than I trusted myself.

Thanks to all these angels, and many others I encountered during those important early years, I received enough strength to remain on the covenant path as I gained a spiritual witness of the truth.

And by the way, that young angel girl, Mônica? After we both served missions, she became my wife.

I don't think it was a coincidence that good friends, Church responsibilities, and nurturing by the good word of God were part of that process. President Gordon B. Hinckley wisely taught: "It is not an easy thing to make the transition incident to joining this Church. It means cutting old ties. It means leaving friends. It may mean setting aside cherished beliefs. It may require a change of habits and a suppression of appetites. In so many cases it means loneliness and even fear of the unknown. There must be nurturing and strengthening during this difficult season of a convert's life" ("There Must Be Messengers," *Ensign,* Oct. 1987, 5).

Later he also taught, "Every one of them needs three things: a friend, a responsibility, and nurturing with 'the good word of God'" ("Converts and Young Men," *Ensign,* May 1997, 47).

Why am I sharing these experiences with you?

First, it is to send a message to those going through a similar process right now. Maybe you are a new convert, or coming back to the Church after wandering around for a while, or just someone struggling to fit in. Please, please, do not give up on your efforts to be part of this big family. It is the true Church of Jesus Christ!

When it comes to your happiness and salvation, it is always worth the effort to keep trying. It is worth the effort to adjust your lifestyle and traditions. The Lord is aware of the challenges you face. He knows you, He loves you, and I promise, He will send angels to help you.

In His own words the Savior said: "I will go before your face. I will be on your right hand and on your left, and my Spirit shall be in your [heart], and mine angels round about you, to bear you up" (Doctrine and Covenants 84:88).

My second purpose for sharing these experiences is to send a message to all members of the Church—to all of us. We should remember that it is not easy for new converts, returning friends, and those with a different lifestyle to instantly fit in. The Lord is aware of the challenges they face, and He is looking for angels willing to help. The Lord is always looking for willing volunteers to be angels in others' lives.

Brothers and sisters, would you be willing to be an instrument in the Lord's hands? Would you be willing to be one of these angels? To be an emissary, sent from God, from this side of the veil, for someone He is worried about? He needs you. They need you.

Of course, we can always count on our missionaries. They are always there, the first ones to enlist for this angelic job. But they are not enough.

If you look around carefully, you will find many in need of an angel's help. These people may not be wearing white shirts, dresses, or any standard Sunday attire. They may be sitting alone, toward the back of the chapel or classroom, sometimes feeling as if they are invisible. Maybe their hairstyle is a little extreme or their vocabulary is different, but they are there, and they are trying.

Some may be wondering, "Should I keep coming back? Should I keep trying?" Others may be wondering if one day they will feel accepted and loved. Angels are needed, right now; angels who are willing to leave their comfort zone to embrace them; "[people who are] so good and so pure that *angelic* is the only word that comes to mind [to describe them]" (Jeffrey R. Holland, "The Ministry of Angels," 30).

Brothers and sisters, I believe in angels! We are all here today, a giant army of angels set apart for these latter days, to minister to others as extensions of the hands of a loving Creator. I promise that if we are willing to serve, the Lord will give us opportunities to be ministering angels. He knows who needs angelic help, and He will put them in our path. The Lord puts those who need angelic help in our path daily.

I am so grateful for the many angels that the Lord has put in my path throughout my life. They were needed. I am also grateful for His gospel that helps us to change and gives us the chance to be better.

This is a gospel of love, a gospel of ministering. Of this I testify in the name of Jesus Christ, amen.

WE TALK OF CHRIST

ELDER NEIL L. ANDERSEN
Of the Quorum of the Twelve Apostles

I express my love for you, our beloved friends and fellow believers. I have admired your faith and courage during these past months, as this worldwide pandemic has disrupted our lives and taken precious family members and dear friends.

During this period of uncertainty, I have felt an unusual gratitude for my sure and certain knowledge that Jesus is the Christ. Have you felt that way? There are difficulties that weigh upon each of us, but always before us is He who humbly declared, "I am the way, the truth, and the life."[1] While we endure a season of physically distancing ourselves from others, we need never endure a season of spiritually distancing ourselves from Him who lovingly calls to us, "Come unto me."[2]

Like a guiding star in a clear, dark sky, Jesus Christ lights our way. He came to earth in a humble stable. He lived a perfect life. He healed the sick and raised the dead. He was a friend to the forgotten. He taught us to do good, to obey, and to love one another. He was crucified on a cross, rising majestically three days later, allowing us and those we love to live beyond the grave. With His incomparable mercy and grace, He took upon Himself our sins and our suffering, bringing forgiveness as we repent and peace in the storms of life. We love Him. We worship Him. We follow Him. He is the anchor of our souls.

Interestingly, while this spiritual conviction is increasing within us, there are many on the earth who know very little of Jesus Christ, and in some parts of the world where His name has been proclaimed for centuries, faith in Jesus Christ is diminishing. The valiant Saints in Europe have seen belief decline in their countries through the decades.[3] Sadly, here in the United States faith is also receding. A recent study revealed that in the last 10 years, 30 million people in the United States have stepped away from believing in the divinity of Jesus Christ.[4] Looking worldwide, another study predicts that in the decades ahead, more than twice as many will leave Christianity as will embrace it.[5]

We, of course, revere the right of each to choose, yet our Heavenly Father declared, "This is my beloved Son: hear him."[6] I witness that the day will come when every knee will bow and every tongue confess that Jesus is the Christ.[7]

How are we to respond to our changing world? While some are neglecting their faith, others are searching for the truth. We have taken upon ourselves the name of the Savior. What more are we to do?

The Preparation of President Russell M. Nelson

Part of our answer may come as we remember how the Lord tutored President Russell M. Nelson in the months prior to his call as President of the Church. Speaking one year before his call, President Nelson invited us to more deeply study the 2,200 references of the name *Jesus Christ* listed in the Topical Guide.[8]

Three months later, in April general conference, he spoke of how, even with his decades of devoted discipleship, this deeper study of Jesus Christ had greatly affected him. Sister Wendy Nelson asked him about its impact. He replied, "I am a different man!" He was a different man? At age 92, a different man? President Nelson explained:

"As we invest time in learning about the Savior and His atoning sacrifice, we are drawn to [Him]. . . .

". . . Our focus [becomes] riveted on the Savior and His gospel."[9]

The Savior said, "Look unto me in every thought."[10]

In a world of work, worries, and worthy endeavors, we keep our heart, our mind, and our thoughts on Him who is our hope and salvation.

If a renewed study of the Savior helped prepare President Nelson, could it not help prepare us as well?

In emphasizing the name of the Church, President Nelson taught, "If we . . . are to have access to the power of the Atonement of Jesus Christ—to cleanse and heal us, to strengthen and magnify us, and ultimately to exalt us—we must clearly acknowledge Him as the source of that power."[11] President Nelson taught us that consistently using the correct name of the Church, something that might seem like a small thing, is not small at all and will shape the world's future.

A Promise for Your Preparation

I promise you that as you prepare yourselves, as President Nelson did, you too will be different, thinking more about the Savior, speaking of Him more frequently and with less hesitation. As you come to know and love Him even more deeply, your words will flow more comfortably, as they do when you speak of one of your children or of a dear friend. Those listening to you will feel less like debating or dismissing you and more like learning from you.

You and I speak of Jesus Christ, but maybe we can do a little better. If the world is going to speak less of Him, who is going to speak more of Him? We are! Along with other devoted Christians!

Speaking of Christ in Our Homes

Are there images of the Savior in our homes? Do we talk often to our children about the parables of Jesus? "The stories of Jesus [are] like a rushing wind across the embers of faith in the hearts of our children."[12] When your children ask you questions, consciously think about teaching what the Savior taught. For example, if your child asks, "Daddy, why do we pray?" You might respond, "That's a great question. Do you remember when Jesus prayed? Let's talk about why He prayed and how He prayed."

"We talk of Christ, we rejoice in Christ, . . . that our children may know to what source they may look for a remission of their sins."[13]

Speaking of Christ in the Church

This same scripture adds that "we preach of Christ."[14] In our worship services, let us focus on the Savior Jesus Christ and the gift of His atoning sacrifice. This does not mean we cannot tell an experience from our own life or share thoughts from others. While our subject might be about families or service or temples or a recent mission, everything in our worship should point to the Lord Jesus Christ.

Thirty years ago, President Dallin H. Oaks spoke of a letter he had received "from a man who said he had attended [a sacrament] meeting and listened to seventeen testimonies without hearing the Savior mentioned."[15] President Oaks then noted, "Perhaps that description is exaggerated [but] I quote it because it provides a vivid reminder for all of us."[16] He then invited us to speak more of Jesus Christ in our talks and class discussions. I have observed that we are focusing more and more on Christ in our Church meetings. Let's consciously continue with these very positive efforts.

Speaking of Christ with Others

With those around us, let us be more open, more willing to talk of Christ. President Nelson said, "True disciples of Jesus Christ are willing to stand out, speak up, and be different from the people of the world."[17]

Sometimes we think that a conversation with someone needs to result in them coming to church or seeing the missionaries. Let the Lord guide them as they are willing, while we think more about our responsibility to be a voice for Him, thoughtful and open about our faith. Elder Dieter F. Uchtdorf has taught us that when someone asks us about our weekend, we should be willing to happily respond that we loved hearing the Primary children sing, "I'm trying to be like Jesus."[18] Let us kindly witness our faith in Christ. If someone shares a problem in his or her personal life, we might say, "John, Mary, you know that I believe in Jesus Christ. I have been thinking about something He said that might help you."

Be more open on social media in talking about your trust in Christ. Most will respect your faith, but if someone is dismissive when you speak of the Savior, take courage in His promise: "Blessed are ye, when men shall revile you . . . for my sake. . . . For great is your reward in heaven."[19] We care more about being His followers than being "liked" by our own followers. Peter counseled, "Be ready always to give an answer [for] the hope that is in you."[20] Let us talk of Christ.

The Book of Mormon is a powerful witness of Jesus Christ. Virtually every page testifies of the Savior and His divine mission.[21] An understanding of His Atonement and grace saturates its pages. As a companion to the New Testament, the Book of Mormon helps us better understand why the Savior came to rescue us and how we can more profoundly come unto Him.

Some of our fellow Christians are, at times, uncertain about our beliefs and motives. Let us genuinely rejoice with them in our shared faith in Jesus Christ and in the New Testament scriptures we all love. In the days ahead, those who believe in Jesus Christ will need the friendship and support of one another.[22]

As the world speaks less of Jesus Christ, let us speak more of Him. As our true colors as His disciples are revealed, many around us will be prepared to listen. As we share the light we have received from Him, His light and His transcendent saving power will shine on those willing to open their hearts. Jesus said, "I . . . come [as] a light into the world."[23]

Lifting Our Desire to Speak of Christ

Nothing lifts my desire to speak of Christ more than visualizing His return. While we do not know when He will come, the events of His return will be breathtaking! He will come in the clouds of heaven in majesty and glory with all His holy angels. Not just a few angels but *all* His holy angels. These are not the cherry-cheeked cherubim painted by Raphael, found on our Valentine cards. These are the angels of the centuries, the angels sent to shut the mouths of lions,[24] to open prison doors,[25] to announce His long-awaited birth,[26] to comfort Him in Gethsemane,[27] to assure His disciples at His Ascension,[28] and to open the glorious Restoration of the gospel.[29]

Can you imagine being caught up to meet Him, whether on this side or the other side of the veil?[30] That is His promise to the righteous. This amazing experience will mark our souls forever.

How grateful we are for our beloved prophet, President Russell M. Nelson, who has lifted our desire to love the Savior and proclaim His divinity. I am an eyewitness to the Lord's hand upon him and the gift of revelation that guides him. President Nelson, we eagerly await your counsel.

My dear friends across the world, let us talk of Christ, anticipating His glorious promise: "Whosoever . . . shall confess me before men, him will I confess . . . before my Father."[31] I testify He is the Son of God. In the name of Jesus Christ, amen.

Notes

1. John 14:6.
2. Matthew 11:28.
3. See Niztan Peri-Rotem, "Religion and Fertility in Western Europe: Trends across Cohorts in Britain, France and the Netherlands," *European Journal of Population*, May 2016, 231–65, ncbi.nlm.nih.gov/pmc/articles/PMC4875064.
4. "[Sixty-five percent] of American adults describe themselves as Christians when asked about their religion, down 12 percentage points over the past decade. Meanwhile, the religiously unaffiliated share of the population, consisting of people who describe their religious identity as atheist, agnostic or 'nothing in particular,' now stands at 26%, up from 17% in 2009" (Pew Research Center, "In U.S., Decline of Christianity Continues at Rapid Pace," Oct. 17, 2019, pewforum.org).
5. See Pew Research Center, "The Future of World Religions: Population Growth Projections, 2010–2050," Apr. 2, 2015, pewforum.org.
6. Mark 9:7; Luke 9:35; see also Matthew 3:17; Joseph Smith—History 1:17.
7. See Philippians 2:9–11.
8. See Russell M. Nelson, "Prophets, Leadership, and Divine Law" (worldwide devotional for young adults, Jan. 8, 2017), broadcasts.ChurchofJesusChrist.org.
9. Russell M. Nelson, "Drawing the Power of Jesus Christ into Our Lives," *Ensign* or *Liahona*, May 2017, 40–41.
10. Doctrine and Covenants 6:36.
11. Russell M. Nelson, "The Correct Name of the Church," *Ensign* or *Liahona*, Nov. 2018, 88.
12. Neil L. Andersen, "Tell Me the Stories of Jesus," *Ensign* or *Liahona*, May 2010, 108.
13. 2 Nephi 25:26.
14. 2 Nephi 25:26.
15. Dallin H. Oaks, "Another Testament of Jesus Christ" (Brigham Young University fireside, June 6, 1993), 7, speeches.byu.edu.
16. Dallin H. Oaks, "Witnesses of Christ," *Ensign*, Nov. 1990, 30.
17. Russell M. Nelson, "Drawing the Power of Jesus Christ into Our Lives," 40.
18. See Dieter F. Uchtdorf, "Missionary Work: Sharing What Is in Your Heart," *Ensign* or *Liahona*, May 2019, 17; "I'm Trying to Be like Jesus," *Children's Songbook*, 78.
19. Matthew 5:11–12.
20. 1 Peter 3:15.
21. "As [the Book of Mormon prophetic scribes] wrote their testimonies of the promised Messiah, they mentioned some form of his name on an average of every 1.7 verses. [They] referred to Jesus Christ by, literally, 101 different names. . . . When we realize that a verse usually consists of one sentence, it appears that we cannot, on the average, read two sentences in the Book of Mormon without seeing some form of Christ's name" (Susan Easton Black, *Finding Christ through the Book of Mormon* [1987], 5, 15).

    "While the words *atone* or *atonement*, in any of their forms, appear only once in the King James translation of the New Testament, they appear 35 times in the Book of Mormon. As another testament of Jesus Christ, it sheds precious light on His Atonement" (Russell M. Nelson, "The Atonement," *Ensign*, Nov. 1996, 35).

22. Those leaving Christianity in the United States are younger. "More than eight-in-ten members of the Silent Generation (those born between 1928 and 1945) describe themselves as Christians (84%), as do three-quarters of Baby Boomers (76%). In stark contrast, only half of Millennials (49%) describe themselves as Christians; four-in-ten are religious 'nones,' and one-in-ten Millennials identify with non-Christian faiths" ("In U.S., Decline of Christianity Continues," pewforum.org).
23. John 12:46.
24. See Daniel 6:22.
25. See Acts 5:19.
26. See Luke 2:2–14.
27. See Luke 22:42–43.
28. See Acts 1:9–11.
29. See Doctrine and Covenants 13; 27:12–13; 110:11–16; Joseph Smith—History 1:27–54.
30. See 1 Thessalonians 4:16–17; Doctrine and Covenants 88:96–98.
31. Matthew 10:32.

LET GOD PREVAIL

PRESIDENT RUSSELL M. NELSON
President of The Church of Jesus Christ of Latter-day Saints

My dear brothers and sisters, how grateful I am for the marvelous messages of this conference and for my privilege to speak with you now.

For the more than 36 years I've been an Apostle, the doctrine of the gathering of Israel has captured my attention.[1] *Everything* about it has intrigued me, including the ministries and names[2] of Abraham, Isaac, and Jacob; their lives and their wives; the covenant God made with them and extended through their lineage;[3] the dispersion of the twelve tribes; and the numerous prophecies about the gathering in our day.

I have studied the gathering, prayed about it, feasted upon every related scripture, and asked the Lord to increase my understanding.

So imagine my delight when I was led recently to a new insight. With the help of two Hebrew scholars, I learned that one of the Hebraic meanings of the word *Israel* is "let God prevail."[4] Thus the very name of *Israel* refers to a person who is *willing* to let God prevail in his or her life. That concept stirs my soul!

The word *willing* is crucial to this interpretation of *Israel.*[5] We all have our agency. We can choose to be of Israel, or not. We can choose to let God prevail in our lives, or not. We can choose to let God be the most powerful influence in our lives, or not.

For a moment, let us recall a crucial turning point in the life of Jacob, the grandson of Abraham. At the place Jacob named *Peniel* (which means "the face of God"),[6] Jacob wrestled with a serious challenge. His agency was tested. Through this wrestle, Jacob proved what was most important to him. He demonstrated that he was willing to let God prevail in his life. In response, God changed Jacob's name to *Israel,*[7] meaning "let God prevail." God then promised Israel that *all* the blessings that had been pronounced upon Abraham's head would also be his.[8]

Sadly, Israel's posterity broke their covenants with God. They stoned the prophets and were *not* willing to let God prevail in their lives. Subsequently, God scattered them to the four corners of the earth.[9] Mercifully, He later promised to gather them, as reported by Isaiah: "For a small moment have I forsaken thee [Israel]; but with great mercies will I gather thee."[10]

With the Hebraic definition of *Israel* in mind, we find that the gathering of Israel takes on added meaning. The Lord is gathering those who are willing to let God prevail in their lives. The Lord is gathering those who will choose to let God be the most important influence in their lives.

For centuries, prophets have foretold this gathering,[11] and it is happening right now! As an essential prelude to the Second Coming of the Lord, it is *the most* important work in the world!

This premillennial gathering is an individual saga of expanding faith and spiritual courage for millions of people. And as members of The Church of Jesus Christ of Latter-day Saints, or "latter-day covenant Israel,"[12] we have been charged to assist the Lord with this pivotal work.[13]

When we speak of gathering Israel on both sides of the veil, we are referring, of course, to missionary, temple, and family history work. We are also referring to building faith and testimony in the hearts of those with whom we live, work, and serve. Anytime we do anything that helps anyone—on either side of the veil—to make and keep their covenants with God, we are helping to gather Israel.

Not long ago, the wife of one of our grandsons was struggling spiritually. I will call her "Jill." Despite fasting, prayer, and priesthood blessings, Jill's father was dying. She was gripped with fear that she would lose both her dad and her testimony.

Late one evening, my wife, Sister Wendy Nelson, told me of Jill's situation. The next morning Wendy felt impressed to share with Jill that my response to her spiritual wrestle was one word! The word was *myopic*.

Jill later admitted to Wendy that initially she was devastated by my response. She said, "I was hoping for Grandfather to promise me a miracle for my dad. I kept wondering why the word *myopic* was the one he felt compelled to say."

After Jill's father passed on, the word *myopic* kept coming to her mind. She opened her heart to understand even more deeply that *myopic* meant "nearsighted." And her thinking began to shift. Jill then said, "*Myopic* caused me to stop, think, and heal. That word now fills me with peace. It reminds me to expand my perspective and seek the eternal. It reminds me that there is a divine plan and that my dad still lives and loves and looks out for me. *Myopic* has led me to God."

I am very proud of our precious granddaughter-in-law. During this heart-wrenching time in her life, dear Jill is learning to embrace God's will for her dad, with an eternal perspective for her own life. By *choosing* to let God prevail, she is finding peace.

If we will allow it, there are many ways this Hebraic interpretation of *Israel* can help us. Imagine how our prayers for our missionaries—and for our own efforts to gather Israel—could change with this concept in mind. We often pray that we and the missionaries will be led to those who are prepared to receive the truths of the restored gospel of Jesus Christ. I wonder, to whom will we be led when we plead to find those who are willing to let God prevail in their lives?

We may be led to some who have never believed in God or Jesus Christ but who are now yearning to learn about Them and Their plan of happiness. Others may have been "born in the covenant"[14] but have since wandered away from the covenant path. They may now be ready to repent, return, and let God prevail. We can assist them by welcoming them with open arms and hearts. And some to whom we may be led may have always felt there was something missing in their lives. They too are longing for the wholeness and joy that come to those who are willing to let God prevail in their lives.

The gospel net to gather scattered Israel is expansive. There is room for each person who will fully embrace the gospel of Jesus Christ. Each convert becomes one of God's covenant children,[15] whether by birth or by adoption. Each becomes a full heir to all that God has promised the faithful children of Israel![16]

Each of us has a divine potential because each is a child of

God. Each is equal in His eyes. The implications of this truth are profound. Brothers and sisters, please listen carefully to what I am about to say. God does not love one race more than another. His doctrine on this matter is clear. He invites *all* to come unto Him, "black and white, bond and free, male and female."[17]

I assure you that your standing before God is not determined by the color of your skin. Favor or disfavor with God is dependent upon your devotion to God and His commandments and not the color of your skin.

I grieve that our Black brothers and sisters the world over are enduring the pains of racism and prejudice. Today I call upon our members everywhere to lead out in abandoning attitudes and actions of prejudice. I plead with you to promote respect for all of God's children.

The question for each of us, regardless of race, is the same. Are *you* willing to let God prevail in your life? Are *you* willing to let God be the most important influence in your life? Will you allow His words, His commandments, and His covenants to influence what you do each day? Will you allow His voice to take priority over any other? Are you *willing* to let whatever He needs you to do take precedence over every other ambition? Are you *willing* to have your will swallowed up in His?[18]

Consider how such willingness could bless you. If you are unmarried and seeking an eternal companion, your desire to be "of Israel" will help you decide whom to date and how.

If you are married to a companion who has broken his or her covenants, your willingness to let God prevail in your life will allow your covenants with God to remain intact. The Savior will heal your broken heart. The heavens will open as you seek to know how to move forward. You do not need to wander or wonder.

If you have sincere questions about the gospel or the Church, as you choose to let God prevail, you will be led to find and understand the absolute, eternal truths that will guide your life and help you stay firmly on the covenant path.

When you are faced with temptation—even if the temptation

comes when you are exhausted or feeling alone or misunderstood—imagine the courage you can muster as you choose to let God prevail in your life and as you plead with Him to strengthen you.

When your greatest desire is to let God prevail, to be part of Israel, so many decisions become easier. So many issues become nonissues! You know how best to groom yourself. You know what to watch and read, where to spend your time, and with whom to associate. You know what you want to accomplish. You know the kind of person you really want to become.

Now, my dear brothers and sisters, it takes both faith and courage to let God prevail. It takes persistent, rigorous spiritual work to repent and to put off the natural man through the Atonement of Jesus Christ.[19] It takes consistent, daily effort to develop personal habits to study the gospel, to learn more about Heavenly Father and Jesus Christ, and to seek and respond to personal revelation.

During these perilous times of which the Apostle Paul prophesied,[20] Satan is no longer even *trying* to hide his attacks on God's plan. Emboldened evil abounds. Therefore, the only way to survive spiritually is to be determined to let God prevail in our lives, to learn to hear His voice, and to use our energy to help gather Israel.

Now, how does the Lord *feel* about people who will let God prevail? Nephi summed it up well: "[The Lord] *loveth* those who will have him to be their God. Behold, he loved our fathers, and he covenanted with them, yea, even Abraham, Isaac, and Jacob; and he remember[s] the covenants which he [has] made."[21]

And what is the Lord willing to *do* for Israel? The Lord has pledged that He will "fight [our] battles, and [our] children's battles, and our children's children's [battles] . . . to the third and fourth generation"![22]

As you study your scriptures during the next six months, I encourage you to make a list of all that the Lord has promised He will do for covenant Israel. I think you will be astounded! Ponder these promises. Talk about them with your family and friends. Then live and watch for these promises to be fulfilled in your own life.

My dear brothers and sisters, as you choose to let God prevail in your lives, you will experience for yourselves that our God is "a God of miracles."[23] As a people, we are His covenant children, and we will be called by His name. Of this I testify in the sacred name of Jesus Christ, amen.

Notes

1. I have spoken of Israel in at least 378 of the more than 800 messages I have delivered during my 36 years as an Apostle.
2. In Hebrew, *Abram* is a noble name meaning "exalted father." But when God changed that name to *Abraham*, the name took on even greater significance, meaning "father of a multitude." Indeed, Abraham was to be the "father of many nations." (See Genesis 17:5; Nehemiah 9:7.)
3. The Lord God Jehovah made a covenant with Abraham that the Savior of the world would be born through Abraham's seed, certain lands would be inherited, and all nations would be blessed through Abraham's lineage (see Bible Dictionary, "Abraham, covenant of").
4. See Bible Dictionary, "Israel."
5. The word *Israel* appears more than a thousand times in the scriptures. It can apply to Jacob's (Israel's) family of 12 sons, plus daughters (see Genesis 35:23–26; 46:7). Today it can apply geographically as a place on planet Earth. But its doctrinal use applies to people who are willing to let God prevail in their lives.
6. See Genesis 32:30; also spelled as *Penuel* in Genesis 32:31.
7. See Genesis 32:28.
8. See Genesis 35:11–12.
9. For further study, see Topical Guide, "Israel, Scattering of."
10. Isaiah 54:7.
11. See Isaiah 11:11–12; 2 Nephi 21:11–12; Mosiah 15:11.
12. See *Encyclopedia of Mormonism* (1992), "Covenant Israel, Latter-Day," 1:330–31.
13. As we participate in the gathering of Israel, the Lord has a wonderful way of describing those being gathered. He refers to us collectively as His "peculiar treasure" (Exodus 19:5; Psalm 135:4), as His "jewels" (Malachi 3:17; Doctrine and Covenants 101:3), and as a "holy nation" (Exodus 19:6; see also Deuteronomy 14:2; 26:18).
14. This phrase refers to the very covenant that God made with Abraham, saying, "In thy seed shall all the kindreds of the earth be blessed" (3 Nephi 20:27). "Born in the covenant" means that before a person was born, that person's mother and father were sealed in the temple.
15. Such a promise was taught by God to Abraham: "As many as receive this Gospel shall be called after thy name, and shall be accounted thy seed, and shall rise up and bless thee, as their father" (Abraham 2:10; see also Romans 8:14–17; Galatians 3:26–29).
16. Each faithful member may request a patriarchal blessing. Through the inspiration of the Holy Ghost, the patriarch declares that person's lineage in the house of Israel. That declaration is not necessarily a pronouncement of his or her race, nationality, or genetic makeup. Rather, the declared lineage identifies the tribe of Israel through which that individual will receive his or her blessings.
17. 2 Nephi 26:33.
18. See Mosiah 15:7. Being of Israel is not for the faint of heart. To receive all the blessings that God has in store for Abraham's seed, we can each expect to be given our own unique "Abrahamic test." God will test us, as the Prophet Joseph Smith taught, by wrenching our very heartstrings. (See recollection of John Taylor in *Teachings of Presidents of the Church: Joseph Smith* [2007], 231.)
19. See Mosiah 3:19.
20. See 2 Timothy 3:1–13.
21. 1 Nephi 17:40; emphasis added.
22. Doctrine and Covenants 98:37; see also Psalm 31:23; Isaiah 49:25; Doctrine and Covenants 105:14.
23. Mormon 9:11.

SUNDAY AFTERNOON SESSION

OCTOBER 4, 2020

TESTED, PROVED, AND POLISHED

PRESIDENT HENRY B. EYRING

Second Counselor in the First Presidency

My dear brothers and sisters, I am grateful to speak with you today. My hope is to give encouragement when life seems especially difficult and uncertain. For some of you, that time is now. If not, such a time will come.

That is not a gloomy view. It is realistic—yet optimistic—because of God's purpose in the Creation of this world. That purpose was to give His children the opportunity to prove themselves able and willing to choose the right when it is hard. In so doing, their natures would be changed and they could become more like Him. He knew that would require unshakable faith in Him.

Much of what I know came from my family. When I was about eight years old, my wise mother asked my brother and me to pull weeds with her in our family's backyard garden. Now, that seems a simple task, but we lived in New Jersey. It rained often. The soil was heavy clay. The weeds grew faster than the vegetables.

I remember my frustration when the weeds broke off in my hands, their roots stuck firmly in the heavy mud. My mother and my brother were soon far ahead in their rows. The harder I tried, the more I fell behind.

"This is too hard!" I cried out.

Instead of giving sympathy, my mother smiled and said, "Oh, Hal, of course it's hard. It's supposed to be. Life is a test."

In that moment, I knew her words were true and would continue to be true in my future.

The reason for Mother's loving smile became clear years later when I read of Heavenly Father and His Beloved Son speaking of Their purpose in creating this world and giving spirit children the opportunity of mortal life:

"And we will prove them herewith, to see if they will do all things whatsoever the Lord their God shall command them;

"And they who keep their first estate shall be added upon; and they who keep not their first estate shall not have glory in the same kingdom with those who keep their first estate; and they who keep their second estate shall have glory added upon their heads for ever and ever."[1]

You and I accepted that invitation to be tested and to prove that we would choose to keep the commandments of God when we would no longer be in the presence of our Heavenly Father.

Even with such a loving invitation from our Heavenly Father, Lucifer persuaded a third of the spirit children to follow him and reject the Father's plan for our growth and eternal happiness. For Satan's rebellion, he was cast out with his followers. Now he tries to cause as many as he can to turn away from God during this mortal life.

Those of us who accepted the plan did so because of our faith in Jesus Christ, who offered to become our Savior and Redeemer. We must have believed then that whatever mortal weaknesses we would have and whatever evil forces would be against us, the forces of good would be overwhelmingly greater.

Heavenly Father and Jesus Christ know and love you. They want you to return to Them and become like Them. Your success is Their success. You have felt that love confirmed by the Holy Ghost when you have read or heard these words: "For behold, this is my work and my glory—to bring to pass the immortality and eternal life of man."[2]

God has the power to make our way easier. He fed manna to the children of Israel in their wandering to the promised land. The Lord in His mortal ministry healed the sick, raised the dead, and calmed the sea. After His Resurrection, He opened "the prison to them that were bound."[3]

Yet the Prophet Joseph Smith, one of the greatest of His prophets, suffered in prison and was taught the lesson we all profit from and need in our recurring tests of faith: "And if thou shouldst be cast into the pit, or into the hands of murderers, and the sentence of death passed upon thee; if thou be cast into the deep; if the billowing surge conspire against thee; if fierce winds become thine enemy; if the heavens gather blackness, and all the elements combine to hedge up the way; and above all, if the very jaws of hell shall gape open the mouth wide after thee, know thou, my son, that all these things shall give thee experience, and shall be for thy good."[4]

You might reasonably wonder why a loving and all-powerful God allows our mortal test to be so hard. It is because He knows that we must grow in spiritual cleanliness and stature to be able to live in His presence in families forever. To make that possible, Heavenly Father gave us a Savior and the power to choose for ourselves by faith to keep His commandments and to repent and so come unto Him.

The Father's plan of happiness has at its center our becoming ever more like His Beloved Son, Jesus Christ. In all things, the Savior's example is our best guide. He was not exempt from the need to prove Himself. He endured for all of Heavenly Father's children, paying the price for all our sins. He felt the suffering of all who have and will come into mortality.

When you wonder how much pain you can endure well, remember Him. He suffered what you suffer so that He would know how to lift you up. He may not remove the burden, but He will give you strength, comfort, and hope. He knows the way. He drank the bitter cup. He endured the suffering of all.

You are being nourished and comforted by a loving Savior, who knows how to succor you in whatever tests you face. Alma taught:

"And he shall go forth, suffering pains and afflictions and temptations of every kind; and this that the word might be fulfilled which saith he will take upon him the pains and the sicknesses of his people.

"And he will take upon him death, that he may loose the bands of death which bind his people; and he will take upon him their infirmities, that his bowels may be filled with mercy, according to the flesh, that he may know according to the flesh how to succor his people according to their infirmities."[5]

One way He will succor you will be to invite you always to remember Him and to come unto Him. He has encouraged us:

"Come unto me, all ye that labour and are heavy laden, and I will give you rest.

"Take my yoke upon you, and learn of me; for I am meek and lowly in heart: and ye shall find rest unto your souls."[6]

The way to come unto Him is to feast upon His words, to exercise faith unto repentance, to choose to be baptized and confirmed by His authorized servant, and then to keep your covenants with God. He sends the Holy Ghost to be your companion, comforter, and guide.

As you live worthy of the gift of the Holy Ghost, the Lord can direct you to safety even when you cannot see the way. For me, He has most often shown the next step or two to take. Rarely has He given me a glimpse of the distant future, but even those infrequent glimpses guide what I choose to do in daily life.

The Lord explained:

"Ye cannot behold with your natural eyes, for the present time, the design of your God concerning those things which shall come hereafter, and the glory which shall follow . . . much tribulation.

"For after much tribulation come the blessings."[7]

The greatest blessing that will come when we prove ourselves faithful to our covenants during our trials will be a change in our natures. By our choosing to keep our covenants, the power of Jesus Christ and the blessings of His Atonement can work in us. Our hearts can be softened to love, to forgive, and to invite others to come unto the Savior. Our confidence in the Lord increases. Our fears decrease.

Now, even with such blessings promised through tribulation, we do not seek tribulation. In the mortal experience, we will have ample opportunity to prove ourselves, to pass tests hard enough to become ever more like the Savior and our Heavenly Father.

In addition, we must notice the tribulation of others and try to help. That will be especially hard when we are being sorely tested ourselves. But we will discover as we lift another's burden, even a little, that our backs are strengthened and we sense a light in the darkness.

In this, the Lord is our Exemplar. On the cross of Golgotha, having already suffered pain so great that He would have died were He not the Begotten Son of God, He looked on His executioners and said to His Father, "Forgive them; for they know not what they do."[8] While suffering for all who would ever live, He looked, from the cross, on John and on His own sorrowing mother and ministered to her in her trial:

"When Jesus therefore saw his mother, and the disciple standing by, whom he loved, he saith unto his mother, Woman, behold thy son!

"Then saith he to the disciple, Behold thy mother! And from that hour that disciple took her unto his own home."[9]

By His actions on that most sacred of days, He voluntarily gave His life for each of us, offering not only succor in this life but eternal life in the time to come.

I have seen people rise to great heights through proving faithful in terrible trials. Across the Church today are examples. People are driven to their knees by adversity. By their faithful endurance and effort, they become more like the Savior and our Heavenly Father.

I learned another lesson from my mother. As a girl she had diphtheria and nearly died. Later she had spinal meningitis. Her father died young, and so my mother and her brothers helped support their mother.

All her life, she felt the effects of the trials of illness. In her last 10 years of life, she required multiple operations. But through it all, she proved faithful to the Lord, even when bedridden. The only picture on her bedroom wall was of the Savior. Her last words to me on her deathbed were these: "Hal, you sound as if you are getting a cold. You ought to take care of yourself."

At her funeral the last speaker was Elder Spencer W. Kimball. After saying something of her trials and her faithfulness, he said essentially this: "Some of you may wonder why Mildred had to suffer so much and so long. I will tell you why. It was because the Lord wanted to polish her a little more."

I express my gratitude for the many faithful members of the Church of Jesus Christ who bear burdens with steady faith and who help others to bear theirs as the Lord seeks to polish them a little more. I also express love and admiration for caregivers and leaders across the world who serve others while they and their families endure such polishing.

I testify that we are children of a Heavenly Father, who loves us. I feel President Russell M. Nelson's love for us all. He is the Lord's prophet in the world today. I so testify in the sacred name of the Lord Jesus Christ, amen.

Notes

1. Abraham 3:25–26.
2. Moses 1:39.
3. Doctrine and Covenants 138:42.
4. Doctrine and Covenants 122:7.
5. Alma 7:11–12.
6. Matthew 11:28–29.
7. Doctrine and Covenants 58:3–4.
8. Luke 23:34.
9. John 19:26–27.

LET PATIENCE HAVE HER PERFECT WORK, AND COUNT IT ALL JOY!

ELDER JEREMY R. JAGGI
Of the Seventy

Two years ago, my youngest brother, Chad, stepped through the veil. His transition to the other side left a hole in the heart of my sister-in-law Stephanie; their two small children, Braden and Bella; as well as the rest of the family. We found comfort in the words of Elder Neil L. Andersen in general conference the week before Chad died: "In the crucible of earthly trials, patiently move forward, and the Savior's healing power will bring you light, understanding, peace, and hope" ("Wounded," *Ensign* or *Liahona,* Nov. 2018, 85).

We have faith in Jesus Christ; we know we will join Chad again, but losing his physical presence hurts! Many have lost loved ones. It is hard to be patient and wait for the time we will rejoin them.

The year after he died, we felt like a dark cloud overshadowed us. We sought refuge in studying our scriptures, praying with more fervency, and attending the temple more frequently. The lines from this hymn capture our feelings at the time: "The day dawn is breaking, the world is awaking, the clouds of night's darkness are fleeing away" ("The Day Dawn Is Breaking," *Hymns,* no. 52).

Our family determined that 2020 would be a refreshing year! We were studying our *Come, Follow Me* lesson in the New Testament book of James in late November 2019 when a theme revealed itself to us. James, chapter 1, verse 2 reads, "My brethren, count it all joy when ye fall into many afflictions" (Joseph Smith Translation, James 1:2 [in James 1:2, footnote *a*]). In our desire to open a new year, a new decade, with joy, we decided that in 2020 we would "count it all joy." We felt so strongly about it that last Christmas we gifted our siblings T-shirts that said in bold letters, "Count It All Joy." The year 2020 would surely be a year of joy and rejoicing.

Well, here we are—2020 instead brought the global COVID-19 pandemic, civil unrest, more natural disasters, and economic challenges. Our Heavenly Father may be allowing us time to reflect and consider our understanding of patience and our conscious decision to choose joy.

The book of James has since taken on new meaning for us. James, chapter 1, verses 3 and 4 continue:

"Knowing this, that the trying of your faith worketh patience.

"But let patience have her perfect work, that ye may be perfect and entire, wanting nothing."

In our efforts to find joy in the midst of our trials, we had forgotten that having patience is the key to letting those trials work for our good.

King Benjamin taught us to put off the natural man and become "a saint through the atonement of Christ the Lord, and [become] as a child, submissive, meek, humble, patient, full of love, willing to submit to all things" (Mosiah 3:19).

Chapter 6 of *Preach My Gospel* teaches key attributes of Christ that we can emulate: "Patience is the capacity to endure delay, trouble, opposition, or suffering without becoming angry, frustrated, or anxious. It is the ability to do God's will and accept His timing. When you are patient, you hold up under pressure and are able to face adversity calmly and hopefully" (*Preach My Gospel: A Guide to Missionary Service,* rev. ed. [2019], 126).

Patience's perfect work may also be illustrated in the life of one of Christ's early disciples, Simon the Canaanite. The Zealots were a group of Jewish nationalists who strongly opposed Roman rule. The Zealot movement advocated violence against the Romans, their Jewish collaborators, and the Sadducees by raiding for provisions and pursuing other activities to aid their cause (see *Encyclopedia Britannica,* "Zealot," britannica.com). Simon the Canaanite was a Zealot (see Luke 6:15). Imagine Simon trying to coax the Savior into taking up arms, leading a militant group, or creating chaos in Jerusalem. Jesus taught:

"Blessed are the meek: for they shall inherit the earth. . . .

"Blessed are the merciful: for they shall obtain mercy. . . .

"Blessed are the peacemakers: for they shall be called the children of God" (Matthew 5:5, 7, 9).

Simon may have embraced and advocated his philosophy with zeal and passion, but the scriptures suggest that through the influence and example of the Savior, his focus changed. His discipleship of Christ became the central focus of his life's efforts.

As we make and keep covenants with God, the Savior can help us to "be born again; yea, born of God, changed from [a] carnal and fallen state, to a state of righteousness, being redeemed of God, becoming his sons and daughters" (Mosiah 27:25).

Of all the zealous social, religious, and political endeavors of our day, let *disciple of Jesus Christ* be our most pronounced and affirming affiliation. "For where your treasure is, there will your heart be also" (Matthew 6:21). Let us also not forget that even after faithful disciples had "done the will of God," they "[had] need of patience" (Hebrews 10:36).

Just as the trying of our faith works patience within us, when we exercise patience, our faith increases. As our faith increases, so does our joy.

This past March, our second daughter, Emma, like many missionaries in the Church, went into mandatory isolation. Many missionaries came home. Many missionaries awaited reassignment. Many did not receive their temple blessings before departing to a field of labor. Thank you, elders and sisters. We love you.

Emma and her companion in the Netherlands were stretched in those first several weeks—stretched to tears in many instances. With only brief opportunities for in-person interaction and limited outdoor exposure, Emma's reliance on God increased. We prayed with her online and asked how we could help. She asked us to connect with friends she was teaching online!

Our family began to connect online, one by one, with Emma's friends in the Netherlands. We invited them to join our weekly, online, extended-family *Come, Follow Me* study. Floor, Laura, Renske, Freek, Benjamin, Stal, and Muhammad all have become our friends. Some of our friends from the Netherlands have entered "in at the strait gate" (3 Nephi 14:13). Others are being shown "the straitness of the path, and the narrowness of the gate, by which they should enter" (2 Nephi 31:9). They are our brothers and sisters in Christ. Each week we "count it all joy" as we work together in our progress on the covenant path.

We "let patience have her perfect work" (James 1:4) in our inability to meet in person as ward families for a season. But we count as joy our families' faith increasing through new technology connections and *Come, Follow Me* study of the Book of Mormon.

President Russell M. Nelson promised, "Your consistent efforts in this endeavor—even during those moments when you feel that you are not being particularly successful—will change your life, that of your family, and the world" ("Go Forward in Faith," *Ensign* or *Liahona,* May 2020, 114).

Where we make sacred covenants with God—the temple—is temporarily closed. Where we keep covenants with God—the home—is open! We have an opportunity at home to study and ponder on the exceptional beauty of temple covenants. Even in the absence of entry into that sacred physical space, our "hearts . . . shall greatly rejoice in consequence of the blessings which shall be poured out" (Doctrine and Covenants 110:9).

Many have lost jobs; others have lost opportunities. We joy, however, alongside President Nelson, who recently stated: "Voluntary fast offerings from our members have actually increased, as well as voluntary contributions to our humanitarian funds. . . . Together we will overcome this difficult time. The Lord will bless you as you continue to bless others" (Russell M. Nelson's Facebook page, post from Aug. 16, 2020, facebook.com/russell.m.nelson).

"Be of good cheer" is the commandment from the Lord, not be of good fear (Matthew 14:27).

Sometimes we get impatient when we think we are "doing everything right" and we still do not receive the blessings we desire. Enoch walked with God for 365 years before he and his people were translated. Three hundred and sixty-five years of striving to do everything right, and then it happened! (See Doctrine and Covenants 107:49.)

My brother Chad's passing came just a few months after our

release from presiding over the Utah Ogden Mission. It was miraculous that while we were living in Southern California, of all the 417 missions we could have been assigned to in the year 2015, we were assigned to northern Utah. The mission home was a 30-minute drive to Chad's home. Chad's cancer was diagnosed after we received our mission assignment. Even in the most trying circumstance, we knew that our Heavenly Father was mindful of us and helping us find joy.

I witness of the redeeming, sanctifying, humbling, and joyous power of the Savior Jesus Christ. I witness that when we pray to our Heavenly Father in the name of Jesus, He will answer us. I witness that as we hear, hearken, and heed the voice of the Lord and His living prophet, President Russell M. Nelson, we can "let patience have her perfect work" and "count it all joy." In the name of Jesus Christ, amen.

HIGHLY FAVORED OF THE LORD

ELDER GARY E. STEVENSON
Of the Quorum of the Twelve Apostles

One day years ago, as young missionaries laboring in a tiny branch on the small island of Amami Oshima, Japan, my companion and I were ecstatic to learn that President Spencer W. Kimball would be visiting Asia and that all members and missionaries in Japan were invited to Tokyo to hear the prophet at an area conference. With branch members, my companion and I excitedly began making plans for the conference, which would require a 12-hour boat ride across the East China Sea to mainland Japan, followed by a 15-hour train ride to Tokyo. Sadly, however, it was not to be. We received word from our mission president that because of distance and time, my companion and I would not be able to attend the conference in Tokyo.

While members of our little branch embarked for Tokyo, we stayed behind. The following days seemed quiet and empty. We held sacrament meeting alone in the small chapel, while the Latter-day Saints and missionaries of Japan attended the conference.

My sense of personal disappointment intensified even as I joyfully listened to branch members return from the conference days later to report that President Kimball had announced a temple in Tokyo. They gushed with excitement as they shared the fulfillment of their dream. They described how, upon hearing the temple announcement, members and missionaries were unable to contain their joy and spontaneously erupted into clapping their hands.

Years have passed, but I can still remember the disappointment I felt from missing that historic meeting.

In recent months I have reflected upon this experience as I have observed others face deep disappointment and sorrow—far greater and deeper than mine ever was as a young missionary—brought on by the worldwide COVID-19 pandemic.

Earlier this year, as the pandemic accelerated, the First Presidency pledged that "the Church and its members will faithfully exhibit our commitment to being good citizens and good neighbors"[1] and will "use an abundance of caution."[2] Thus, we experienced the suspension of Church gatherings worldwide, the return of more than half the Church's missionary force to their home nations, and the closure of all temples throughout the Church. Thousands of you were preparing to enter the temple for living ordinances—including temple sealings. Others of you have completed your service as missionaries early or have been temporarily released and reassigned.

During this time, government and educational leaders closed schools—which consequently altered graduations and forced the cancellation of sporting, social, cultural, and educational events and activities. Many of you prepared for events that were not attended, performances that were not heard, and athletic seasons that were not played.

Even more poignant are thoughts of families who have lost loved ones during this time; most could not hold funerals or other tender gatherings as they had hoped.

In short, many, many of you have dealt with heartbreaking disappointment, sorrow, and discouragement. So how do we heal, endure, and move forward when things seem so broken?

The prophet Nephi began engraving the small plates when he was a grown man. As he looked back on his life and ministry, he offered an important reflection in the very first verse of the Book of Mormon. This verse frames an important principle for us to consider in our time. Following his familiar words, "I, Nephi, having been born of goodly parents . . . ," he writes, "and having seen many afflictions in the course of my days, nevertheless, having been highly favored of the Lord in all my days."[3]

As students of the Book of Mormon, we are familiar with the many afflictions to which Nephi refers. Yet following acknowledgment of his afflictions in the course of his days, Nephi gives his gospel perspective of being highly favored of the Lord in all his days. Times of affliction and disappointment do not change the watchful eye of the Lord as He favorably looks upon us, blessing us.

Lesa and I recently met virtually with about 600 missionaries in

Australia, most of whom were under some measure of confinement or restriction related to COVID-19, many working from their apartments. Together we considered individuals in the New Testament, Book of Mormon, and Doctrine and Covenants whom the Lord blessed to accomplish greatness in adversity. All were defined more by what they were able to do with the Lord's help than by what they could not do as a result of their confinement and restriction.

We read of Paul and Silas, who, while imprisoned in stocks, prayed, sang, taught, testified—and even baptized the jailer.[4]

And again of Paul, in Rome, who was under house arrest for two years, during which time he continually "expounded and testified the kingdom of God,"[5] "teaching those things which concern the Lord Jesus Christ."[6]

Of Nephi and Lehi, the sons of Helaman, who after abuse and imprisonment were encircled by a fire of protection as the Lord's "still voice of perfect mildness . . . did pierce [their captors] even to the very soul."[7]

Of Alma and Amulek in Ammonihah, who found that many "did believe . . . and began to repent, and to search the scriptures,"[8] even though they were then mocked and without food, water, or clothes, bound and confined in prison.[9]

And finally of Joseph Smith, who, while languishing in Liberty Jail, felt abandoned and forsaken, then heard the words of the Lord: "These things . . . shall be for thy good"[10] and "God shall be with you forever."[11]

Each of them understood what Nephi knew: that although they had seen many afflictions in the course of their days, they were highly favored of the Lord.

We too can draw parallels as individual members and as a church in the way in which we have been highly favored of the Lord during the challenging times we have encountered the past several months. As I cite these examples, let them also strengthen your testimony of the seership of our living prophet, who prepared us with adjustments before any hint of a pandemic, enabling us to endure the challenges that have come.

First, **becoming more home centered and Church supported.**

Two years ago, President Russell M. Nelson said: "We have become accustomed to thinking of 'church' as something that happens in our meetinghouses, supported by what happens at home. We need an adjustment to this pattern. . . . A *home-centered Church,* supported by what takes place inside our . . . buildings."[12] What a prophetic adjustment! Home-centered gospel learning has been put into practice with the temporary closure of meetinghouses. Even as the world begins to normalize and we return to chapels, we will want to retain our home-centered patterns of gospel study and learning developed during the pandemic.

A second example of being highly favored of the Lord is the revelation regarding **ministering in a higher and holier way.**

In 2018, President Nelson introduced ministering as an adjustment "in the way we care for each other."[13] The pandemic has introduced numerous opportunities to hone our ministering skills. Ministering brothers and sisters, young women and young men, and others have reached out to provide contact, conversation, yard care, meals, messages via technology, and the sacrament ordinance to bless those in need. The Church itself has also been ministering to others during the pandemic with an unprecedented distribution of commodities to food banks, homeless shelters, and immigrant support centers and with projects directed to the world's most serious hunger situations. Relief Society sisters and their families responded to the challenge of making millions of masks for health-care workers.

A final example of being blessed during adversity is **finding heightened joy in the return of temple ordinances.**

This is best described with a story. When Sister Kaitlyn Palmer received her mission call last April, she was excited to be called as a missionary but felt it equally important and special to go to the temple to receive her endowment and make sacred covenants. Shortly after she scheduled her endowment, the announcement came that all temples would temporarily close due to the worldwide pandemic. After receiving this heartbreaking information, she then learned she would attend the missionary training center (MTC) virtually from her home. Despite these disappointments, Kaitlyn focused on keeping her spirits high.

In the intervening months, Sister Palmer never lost hope of attending the temple. Her family fasted and prayed that temples would open prior to her departure. Kaitlyn would often start her home MTC mornings by saying, "Is today going to be the day we receive a miracle and temples open back up?"

On August 10, the First Presidency announced that Kaitlyn's temple would reopen for living ordinances on the exact day her early-morning flight to her mission was scheduled. She would not be able to attend the temple and make her flight. With little hope for success, her family contacted temple president Michael Vellinga to see if there was any way the miracle they had been praying for could be realized. Their fasting and prayers were answered!

At 2:00 a.m., hours before her flight departure, Sister Palmer and her family, in tears, were greeted at the temple doors by the smiling temple president with the words, "Good morning, Palmer family. Welcome to the temple!" As she completed her endowment, they were encouraged to move quickly, as the next family was waiting at the temple doors. They drove directly to the airport just in time to make her flight to her mission.

The temple ordinances we have missed over several months seem sweeter than previously imagined as temples around the world reopen in phases.

As I close, please listen to the encouraging, enthusiastic, uplifting words of the Prophet Joseph Smith. One would never guess he penned them in affliction and isolation, constrained and restricted at a home in Nauvoo, hiding from those who were seeking to illegally apprehend him:

"Now, what do we hear in the gospel which we have received? A voice of gladness! A voice of mercy from heaven; and a voice of truth out of the earth; glad tidings for the dead; a voice of gladness for the living and the dead; glad tidings of great joy. . . .

". . . Shall we not go on in so great a cause? Go forward and not backward. Courage, . . . and on, on to the victory! Let your hearts rejoice, and be exceedingly glad. Let the earth break forth into singing."[14]

Brothers and sisters, I believe that one day, each of you will look back at the canceled events, the sadness, the disappointments, and the loneliness attendant to the challenging times we are passing through to see them overshadowed by choice blessings and increased faith and testimonies. I believe that in this life, and in the life to come, your afflictions, your Ammonihah, your Liberty Jail, will be consecrated for your gain.[15] I pray that, along with Nephi, we can acknowledge the afflictions in the course of our days while at the same time recognizing that we are highly favored of the Lord.

I close with my testimony of Jesus Christ, who Himself was no stranger to affliction and as part of His infinite Atonement descended below all things.[16] He understands our grief, pain, and desperation. He is our Savior, our Redeemer, our hope, our consolation, and our Deliverer. Of this I testify in His holy name, Jesus Christ, amen.

Notes

1. First Presidency letter, Apr. 16, 2020.
2. First Presidency letter, May 19, 2020.
3. 1 Nephi 1:1.
4. See Acts 16:24–33.
5. Acts 28:23.
6. Acts 28:31.
7. Helaman 5:30.
8. Alma 14:1.
9. See Alma 14:22.
10. Doctrine and Covenants 122:7.
11. Doctrine and Covenants 122:9.
12. Russell M. Nelson, "Opening Remarks," *Ensign* or *Liahona*, Nov. 2018, 7.
13. Russell M. Nelson, "Let Us All Press On," *Ensign* or *Liahona*, May 2018, 118.
14. Doctrine and Covenants 128:19, 22.
15. See 2 Nephi 2:2.
16. See Doctrine and Covenants 122:8.

ASK, SEEK, AND KNOCK

MILTON CAMARGO

First Counselor in the Sunday School General Presidency

Four months ago, in my study of the scriptures, I was reading about Alma's mission in Ammonihah when I came across this suggestion in *Come, Follow Me:* "As you read about the great blessings God gave the people of Nephi (see Alma 9:19–23), ponder the great blessings He has given you."[1] I decided to make a list of God's blessings to me and record it in my digital version of the manual. In a matter of minutes, I had listed 16 blessings.

Foremost among them were the great blessings of the Savior's mercy and atoning sacrifice on my behalf. I also wrote of the blessing I had to represent the Savior as a young missionary in Portugal and, later, with my loving eternal companion, Patricia, in the Brazil Porto Alegre South Mission, where we served with 522 powerful and wonderful missionaries. Speaking of Patricia, many of the blessings I recorded that day are blessings we have enjoyed together throughout our 40 years of marriage—including our sealing in the São Paulo Brazil Temple, our three wonderful children, their spouses, and our 13 grandchildren.

My thoughts turned also to my righteous parents, who raised me in the principles of the gospel. I was reminded in particular of a moment when my loving mother knelt with me to pray by my bedside when I was around 10 years of age. She must have felt that if my prayers were going to reach my Father in Heaven, they would need to improve. So she said, "I will pray first, and after my prayer, you pray." She continued this pattern for many nights, until she was confident I had learned by principle and by practice how to speak to Heavenly Father. I will be forever grateful to her for teaching me to pray, for I learned that my Heavenly Father hears my prayers and answers them.

In fact, that was another blessing that I included in my list—the gift to be able to hear and learn the will of the Lord. An important part of Heavenly Father's plan is the opportunity to communicate with Him anytime we want.

An Invitation from the Lord

When the Savior visited the Americas after His Resurrection, He repeated an invitation that He had given to His disciples in Galilee. He said:

"Ask, and it shall be given unto you; seek, and ye shall find; knock, and it shall be opened unto you.

"For every one that asketh, receiveth; and he that seeketh, findeth; and to him that knocketh, it shall be opened" (3 Nephi 14:7–8; see also Matthew 7:7–8).

Our prophet, President Russell M. Nelson, has given a similar invitation in our day. He said: "Pray in the name of Jesus Christ about your concerns, your fears, your weaknesses—yes, the very longings of your heart. And then listen! Write the thoughts that come to your mind. Record your feelings and follow through with actions that you are prompted to take. As you repeat this process day after day, month after month, year after year, you will 'grow into the principle of revelation.'"[2]

President Nelson added, "In coming days, it will not be possible to survive spiritually without the guiding, directing, comforting, and constant influence of the Holy Ghost."[3]

Why is revelation so essential to our spiritual survival? Because the world can be confusing and noisy, full of deception and distractions. Communication with our Father in Heaven enables us to sort through what is true and what is false, what is relevant to the Lord's plan for us and what is not. The world can also be harsh and heartbreaking. But as we open our hearts in prayer, we will feel the comfort that comes from our Father in Heaven and the assurance that He loves and values us.

Ask

The Lord said that "every one that asketh, receiveth." Asking seems simple, and yet it is powerful because it reveals our desires and our faith. However, it takes time and patience to learn to understand the voice of the Lord. We pay attention to thoughts and feelings that come to our minds and hearts, and we write them down, as our prophet has counseled us to do. Recording our impressions is an important part of receiving. It helps us recall, review, and refeel what the Lord is teaching us.

Recently a loved one said to me, "I believe personal revelation to be true. I believe the Holy Ghost will show me all things I should do.[4] It is easy to believe when I feel my bosom burn with undoubting conviction.[5] But how can I have the Holy Ghost always speak to me at this level?"

To my loved one and to all of you, I would say that I too would like to constantly feel those strong impressions from the Spirit and always see clearly the path to follow. But I don't. However, what we might feel more often is the still, small voice of the Lord whispering to our mind and heart: "I am here. I love you. Go on; do your best. I will support you." We don't always need to know everything or see everything.

The still, small voice is reaffirming, encouraging, and comforting —and many times that's just what we need for the day. The Holy Ghost is real, and His impressions are real—the big ones and the small ones.

Seek

The Lord went on to promise, "He that seeketh, findeth." Seeking implies mental and spiritual effort—pondering, testing, trying, and studying. We seek because we trust the Lord's promises. "For he that cometh to God must believe that he is, and that he is a rewarder of them that diligently seek him" (Hebrews 11:6). When we seek, we are humbly acknowledging that we still have much to learn, and the Lord will expand our understanding, preparing us to receive more. "For behold, thus saith the Lord God: I will give unto the children of men line upon line, precept upon precept, here a little and there a little; . . . for unto him that receiveth I will give more" (2 Nephi 28:30).

Knock

Finally, the Lord said, "To him that knocketh, it shall be opened." To knock is to act in faith. When we actively follow Him, the Lord opens the way before us. There is a beautiful hymn that teaches us to "wake up and do something more than dream of [our] mansion above. Doing good is a pleasure, a joy beyond measure, a blessing of duty and love."[6] Elder Gerrit W. Gong of the Quorum of the Twelve recently explained that revelation often comes while we are in the act of doing good. He said: "As we try to reach out in service to those around us, I think the Lord gives us an extra measure of His love for them and therefore for us. I think we hear His voice—we feel Him in a different way—as we pray to help those around us because that's one of the prayers that He most wants to answer."[7]

Alma's Example

That simple suggestion in *Come, Follow Me* to think about my blessings brought a sweet spirit and some unexpected spiritual insights. As I continued reading about Alma and his ministry in Ammonihah, I discovered that Alma provides a good example of what it means to ask, seek, and knock. We read that "Alma labored much in the spirit, wrestling with God in mighty prayer, that he would pour out his Spirit upon the people." That prayer, however, was not answered the way he hoped, and Alma was cast out of the city. "Weighed down with sorrow," Alma was about to give up, when an angel delivered this message: "Blessed art thou, Alma; therefore, lift up thy head and rejoice, for thou hast great cause to rejoice." The angel then told him to return to Ammonihah and try again, and Alma "returned speedily."[8]

What do we learn from Alma about asking, seeking, and knocking? We learn that prayer requires spiritual labor, and it does not always lead to the outcome we hope for. But when we feel discouraged or weighed down with sorrow, the Lord gives us comfort and strength in different ways. He may not answer all of our questions or solve all of our problems right away; rather, He encourages us to keep trying. If we then speedily align our plan with His plan, He will open the way for us, as He did for Alma.

It is my testimony that this is the dispensation of the fulness of the gospel. We can enjoy the blessings of the Atonement of Jesus Christ in our lives. We have the scriptures widely available to us. We are led by prophets who teach us the will of the Lord for the difficult times we live in. In addition, we have direct access to our own revelation so the Lord can comfort and guide us personally. As the angel said to Alma, we have "great cause to rejoice" (Alma 8:15). In the name of Jesus Christ, amen.

Notes

1. *Come, Follow Me—For Individuals and Families: Book of Mormon 2020* (2019), 91.
2. Russell M. Nelson, "Revelation for the Church, Revelation for Our Lives," *Ensign* or *Liahona*, May 2018, 95; quoting *Teachings of Presidents of the Church: Joseph Smith* (2007), 132.
3. Russell M. Nelson, "Revelation for the Church, Revelation for Our Lives," 96.
4. See 2 Nephi 32:5.
5. See Doctrine and Covenants 9:8.
6. "Have I Done Any Good?" *Hymns*, no. 223.
7. "How I #HearHim: Elder Gerrit W. Gong" (video), ChurchofJesusChrist.org/media.
8. See Alma 8:10–18.

DO JUSTLY, LOVE MERCY, AND WALK HUMBLY WITH GOD

ELDER DALE G. RENLUND
Of the Quorum of the Twelve Apostles

As followers of Jesus Christ, and as Latter-day Saints, we strive—and are encouraged to strive—to do better and be better.[1] Perhaps you have wondered, as I have, "Am I doing enough?" "What else should I be doing?" or "How can I, as a flawed person, qualify to 'dwell with God in a state of never-ending happiness'?"[2]

The Old Testament prophet Micah asked the question this way: "Wherewith shall I come before the Lord, and bow myself before the high God?"[3] Micah satirically wondered whether even exorbitant offerings might be enough to compensate for sin, saying: "Will the Lord be pleased with thousands of rams, or with ten [thousand] . . . rivers of oil? shall I give my firstborn for . . . the sin of my soul?"[4]

The answer is no. Good deeds are not sufficient. Salvation is not earned.[5] Not even the vast sacrifices Micah knew were impossible can redeem the smallest sin. Left to our own devices, the prospect of returning to live in God's presence is hopeless.[6]

Without the blessings that come from Heavenly Father and Jesus Christ, we can never do enough or be enough by ourselves. The good news, though, is that because of and through Jesus Christ we can become enough.[7] All people will be saved from physical death by the grace of God, through the death and Resurrection of Jesus Christ.[8] And if we turn our hearts to God, salvation from spiritual death is available to all "through the Atonement of [Jesus] Christ . . . by obedience to the laws and ordinances of the Gospel."[9] We can be redeemed from sin to stand clean and pure before God. As Micah explained, "[God] hath shewed thee, O man, what is good; and what doth the Lord require of thee, but to do justly, and to love mercy, and to walk humbly with thy God?"[10]

Micah's direction on turning our hearts to God and qualifying for salvation contains three interconnected elements. To *do justly* means acting honorably with God and with other people. We act honorably with God by walking humbly with Him. We act honorably with others by loving mercy. To *do justly* is therefore a practical application of the first and second great commandments, to "love the Lord thy God with all thy heart, and with all thy soul, and with all thy mind . . . [and to] love thy neighbour as thyself."[11]

To *do justly* and *walk humbly with God* is to intentionally withdraw our hand from iniquity, walk in His statutes, and remain authentically faithful.[12] A just person turns away from sin and toward God, makes covenants with Him, and keeps those covenants. A just person chooses to obey the commandments of God, repents when falling short, and keeps on trying.

When the resurrected Christ visited the Nephites, He explained that the law of Moses had been replaced by a higher law. He instructed them not to "offer up . . . sacrifices and . . . burnt offerings" any longer but to offer "a broken heart and a contrite spirit." He also promised, "And whoso cometh unto me with a broken heart and a contrite spirit, him will I baptize with fire and with the Holy Ghost."[13] When we receive and use the gift of the Holy Ghost after baptism, we can enjoy the constant companionship of the Holy Ghost and be taught all things that we should do,[14] including how to walk humbly with God.

Jesus Christ's sacrifice for sin and salvation from spiritual death are available to all who have such a broken heart and contrite spirit.[15] A broken heart and contrite spirit prompt us to joyfully repent and try to become more like our Heavenly Father and Jesus Christ. As we do so, we receive the Savior's cleansing, healing, and strengthening power. We not only do justly and walk humbly with God; we also learn to love mercy the way that Heavenly Father and Jesus Christ do.

God delights in mercy and does not begrudge its use. In Micah's words to Jehovah, "Who is a God like unto thee, that pardoneth iniquity, . . . will have compassion upon us," and will "cast all . . . sins into the depths of the sea."[16] To love mercy as God does is inseparably connected to dealing justly with others and not mistreating them.

The importance of not mistreating others is highlighted in an anecdote about Hillel the Elder, a Jewish scholar who lived in the first century before Christ. One of Hillel's students was exasperated by the complexity of the Torah—the five books of Moses with their 613 commandments and associated rabbinic writings. The student challenged Hillel to explain the Torah using only the time that Hillel could stand on one foot. Hillel may not have had great balance but accepted the challenge. He quoted from Leviticus, saying, "Thou shalt not avenge, nor bear any grudge against the children of thy people, but thou shalt love thy neighbour as thyself."[17] Hillel then concluded: "That which is hateful unto you, do not do to your neighbor. This is the whole of the Torah; the rest is commentary. Go forth and study."[18]

Always dealing honorably with others is part of loving mercy. Consider a conversation I overheard decades ago in the emergency department of Johns Hopkins Hospital in Baltimore, Maryland, in the United States. A patient, Mr. Jackson, was a courteous, pleasant man who was well known to the hospital staff. He had previously been hospitalized multiple times for the treatment of alcohol-related diseases. On this occasion, Mr. Jackson returned to the hospital for symptoms that would be diagnosed as inflammation of the pancreas caused by alcohol consumption.

Toward the end of his shift, Dr. Cohen, a hardworking and admired physician, evaluated Mr. Jackson and determined that hospitalization was warranted. Dr. Cohen assigned Dr. Jones, the physician next up in rotation, to admit Mr. Jackson and oversee his treatment.

Dr. Jones had attended a prestigious medical school and was just beginning her postgraduate studies. This grueling training was often associated with sleep deprivation, which likely contributed to Dr. Jones's negative response. Confronted with her fifth admission of the night, she complained loudly to Dr. Cohen. She felt it was unfair that she would have to spend many hours caring for Mr. Jackson, because his predicament was, after all, self-inflicted.

Dr. Cohen's emphatic response was spoken in almost a whisper. He said, "Dr. Jones, you became a physician to care for people and work to heal them. You didn't become a physician to judge them. If you don't understand the difference, you have no right to train at this institution." Following this correction, Dr. Jones diligently cared for Mr. Jackson during the hospitalization.

Mr. Jackson has since died. Both Dr. Jones and Dr. Cohen have had stellar careers. But at a critical moment in her training, Dr. Jones needed to be reminded to do justly, to love mercy, and to care for Mr. Jackson without being judgmental.[19]

Over the years, I have benefited from that reminder. Loving mercy means that we do not just love the mercy God extends to us; we delight that God extends the same mercy to others. And we follow His example. "All are alike unto God,"[20] and we all need spiritual treatment to be helped and healed. The Lord has said, "Ye shall not esteem one flesh above another, or one man shall not think himself above another."[21]

Jesus Christ exemplified what it means to do justly and to love mercy. He freely associated with sinners, treating them honorably and with respect. He taught the joy of keeping God's commandments and sought to lift rather than condemn those who struggled. He did denounce those who faulted Him for ministering to people they deemed unworthy.[22] Such self-righteousness offended Him and still does.[23]

To be Christlike, a person does justly, behaving honorably with both God and other people. A just person is civil in words and action and recognizes that differences in outlook or belief do not preclude genuine kindness and friendship. Individuals who do justly "will not have a mind to injure one another, but to live peaceably"[24] one with another.

To be Christlike, a person loves mercy. People who love mercy are not judgmental; they manifest compassion for others, especially for those who are less fortunate; they are gracious, kind, and honorable. These individuals treat everyone with love and understanding, regardless of characteristics such as race, gender, religious affiliation, sexual orientation, socioeconomic status, and tribal, clan, or national differences. These are superseded by Christlike love.

To be Christlike, a person chooses God,[25] walks humbly with Him, seeks to please Him, and keeps covenants with Him. Individuals who walk humbly with God remember what Heavenly Father and Jesus Christ have done for them.

Am I doing enough? What else should I be doing? The action we take in response to these questions is central to our happiness in this life and in the eternities. The Savior does not want us to take salvation for granted. Even after we have made sacred covenants, there is a possibility that we may "fall from grace and depart from the living God." So we should "take heed and pray always" to avoid falling "into temptation."[26]

But at the same time, our Heavenly Father and Jesus Christ do not want us to be paralyzed by continual uncertainty during our mortal journey, wondering whether we have done enough to be saved and exalted. They surely do not want us to be tormented by mistakes from which we have repented, thinking of them as wounds that never heal,[27] or to be excessively apprehensive that we might stumble again.

We can assess our own progress. We can know "that the course of life [that we are] pursuing is according to God's will"[28] when we do justly, love mercy, and walk humbly with our God. We assimilate the attributes of Heavenly Father and Jesus Christ into our character, and we love one another.

When you do these things, you will follow the covenant path and qualify to "dwell with God in a state of never-ending happiness."[29] Your souls will be infused with the glory of God and with the light of everlasting life.[30] You will be filled with incomprehensible joy.[31] I testify that God lives and that Jesus is the Christ, our Savior and Redeemer, and He lovingly and joyfully extends His mercy to all. Don't you love it? In the name of Jesus Christ, amen.

Notes

1. See Russell M. Nelson, "We Can Do Better and Be Better," *Ensign* or *Liahona*, May 2019, 67–69.
2. Mosiah 2:41.
3. Micah 6:6.
4. Micah 6:7.

5. See Ephesians 2:8; 2 Nephi 31:19; Alma 22:14; 42:14; 3 Nephi 18:32; Moroni 6:4; Doctrine and Covenants 3:20.
6. See 3 Nephi 27:19.
7. See Alma 41:8; Moroni 10:32–33.
8. See 1 Corinthians 15:22; Alma 11:42–45.
9. Articles of Faith 1:3.
10. Micah 6:8; see similar admonitions in Alma 41:14; Doctrine and Covenants 11:12; Articles of Faith 1:13.
11. See Matthew 22:35–40. For a discussion of the relationship between the first and second great commandments, see Russell M. Nelson, "Teach Us Tolerance and Love," *Ensign*, May 1994, 69–71; Dallin H. Oaks, "Two Great Commandments," *Ensign* or *Liahona*, Nov. 2019, 73–76.
12. See Ezekiel 18:8–9.
13. 3 Nephi 9:19–20; see also Doctrine and Covenants 59:8.
14. See 2 Nephi 32:5.
15. See 2 Nephi 2:7.
16. Micah 7:18–19.
17. Leviticus 19:18.
18. See Babylonian Talmud, Shabbat 31a:6; see also jewishvirtuallibrary.org/rabbi-hillel-quotes-on-judaism-and-israel. Of note, Hillel the Elder was the grandfather of Gamaliel, who is mentioned in Acts 5:34. Gamaliel was the teacher of Saul of Tarsus. See Isidore Singer, ed., *The Jewish Encyclopedia* (1903), "Gamaliel I," 5:558–59.
19. The names for Mr. Jackson, Dr. Cohen, and Dr. Jones are not their own.
20. 2 Nephi 26:33.
21. Mosiah 23:7.
22. See Joseph Smith, "History, 1838–1856, volume D-1 [1 August 1842–1 July 1843]," 1459, josephsmithpapers.org.
23. See Luke 15:1–2.
24. Mosiah 4:13.
25. See Moses 7:33.
26. Doctrine and Covenants 20:32–34.
27. See Boyd K. Packer, "The Plan of Happiness," *Ensign* or *Liahona*, May 2015, 28. President Packer said: "When the repentance process is complete, no scars remain because of the Atonement of Jesus Christ. . . . The Atonement . . . can wash clean every stain no matter how difficult or how long or how many times repeated. The Atonement can put you free again to move forward, cleanly and worthily, to pursue that path that you have chosen in life."
28. *Lectures on Faith* (1985), 38.
29. Mosiah 2:41.
30. See Alma 19:6.
31. See Doctrine and Covenants 11:13.

ENDURING POWER

ELDER KELLY R. JOHNSON
Of the Seventy

In reviewing the teachings of our dear prophet, President Russell M. Nelson, I found a word that he has frequently used in many talks. This word is *power.*

In the first general conference after he was sustained as an Apostle, President Nelson talked about power.[1] He has continued teaching about power over the years. Since we have sustained President Nelson as our prophet, he has taught about the principle of power—specifically, God's power—and how we can access it. He has taught how we can draw upon God's power as we minister to others,[2] how repentance invites the power of Jesus Christ and His Atonement into our lives,[3] and how priesthood—the power and authority of God—blesses all who make and keep covenants with Him.[4] President Nelson has testified that God's power flows to all who are endowed in the temple as they keep their covenants.[5]

I was particularly moved by a challenge President Nelson gave in the April 2020 general conference. He instructed us to "study and pray to learn more about the power and knowledge with which you have been endowed—or with which you will yet be endowed."[6]

In response to this challenge, I have studied and prayed and have learned some beneficial things about the power and knowledge with which I have been endowed—or with which I will yet be endowed.

Understanding what we must do to access God's power in our lives is not easy, but I have found it is doable by studying it out in our minds and praying for the Holy Ghost to enlighten us.[7] Elder Richard G. Scott offered a clear definition of what the power of God is: it is the "power to do more than we can do by ourselves."[8]

Filling our heart and even our soul with the word of God and the foundation of faith in Jesus Christ is crucial to drawing upon the power of God to help us in these challenging times. Without getting the word of God and faith in Jesus Christ deep into our hearts, our testimonies and faith may fail, and we may lose access to the power

God wants to give us. Superficial faith is insufficient. Only faith and the word of God that fill our inner soul are sufficient to sustain us—and to allow us to access His power.

As Sister Johnson and I were raising our children, we encouraged each of them to learn to play a musical instrument. But we would allow our children to take music lessons only if they did their part and practiced their instrument each day. One Saturday, our daughter Jalynn was excited to go play with friends, but she had not yet practiced the piano. Knowing she had committed to practice for 30 minutes, she intended to set a timer because she did not want to practice even one minute longer than was required.

As she walked by the microwave oven on her way to the piano, she paused and pushed some buttons. But instead of setting the timer, she set the microwave to cook for 30 minutes and pushed start. After about 20 minutes of practice, she walked back to the kitchen to check how much time was remaining and found the microwave oven on fire.

She then ran into the backyard where I was doing yard work, yelling that the house was on fire. I quickly ran into the house, and indeed, I found the microwave oven in flames.

In an effort to save our home from burning, I reached behind the microwave, unplugged it, and used the power cord to lift the burning microwave off of the counter. Hoping to be the hero and to save the day as well as our home, I swung the flaming microwave in circles with the power cord to keep it away from my body, got to the backyard, and with another swinging motion flung the microwave out onto the lawn. There we were able to extinguish the fiery flames with a hose.

What had gone wrong? A microwave oven needs something to absorb its energy, and when nothing is on the inside to absorb the energy, the oven itself absorbs the energy, becomes hot, and may catch on fire, destroying itself in a pile of flames and ashes.[9] Our entire microwave went up in flames and burned because there was nothing on the inside.

Likewise, those who have faith and the word of God deep in

their hearts will be able to absorb and overcome the fiery darts that the adversary will surely send to destroy us.[10] Otherwise, our faith, hope, and conviction may not endure, and like the empty microwave oven, we could become a casualty.

I have learned that having the word of God deep in my soul, coupled with faith in the Lord Jesus Christ and His Atonement, allows me to draw upon the power of God to overcome the adversary and anything he may throw at me. As we face challenges, we can rely upon the promise of the Lord taught by Paul: "For God hath not given us the spirit of fear; but of power, and of love, and of a sound mind."[11]

We know that as a child the Savior "grew, and waxed strong in spirit, filled with wisdom: and the grace of God was upon him."[12] We know that as He grew older, "Jesus increased in wisdom and stature, and in favour with God and man."[13] And we know that by the time His ministry commenced, those who heard Him "were astonished at his doctrine: for his word was with power."[14]

Through preparation, the Savior grew in power and was able to resist all of Satan's temptations.[15] As we follow the Savior's example and prepare through studying the word of God and deepening our faith, we also can draw upon the power of God to resist temptations.

During this time of restricted gathering that makes regular temple attendance impossible, I have actually made a point to continue to study and learn more about the power of God that comes to us as we make and keep temple covenants. As promised in the dedicatory prayer of the Kirtland Temple, we leave the temple armed with God's power.[16] There is no expiration date associated with the power God bestows upon those who make and keep temple covenants, nor is there a restriction from accessing that power during a pandemic. His power diminishes in our lives only if we fail to keep our covenants and do not live in a way that allows us to continually qualify to receive His power.

While my dear wife and I were serving as mission leaders in Thailand, Laos, and Myanmar, we witnessed firsthand the power of God that comes to those who make and keep sacred covenants in the temple. The Temple Patron Assistance Fund made it possible for many Saints in these three countries to attend the temple after doing all they could through personal sacrifice and preparation. I recall meeting a group of 20 faithful Saints from Laos at an airport in Bangkok, Thailand, to help them transfer to another airport in Bangkok to catch their flight to Hong Kong. These members were brimming with excitement to finally be traveling to the house of the Lord.

When we met these good Saints upon their return, the added gospel maturity and associated power resulting from receiving their temple endowment and entering into covenants with God were evident. These Saints clearly went forth from the temple "armed with [His] power."[17] This power to do more than they could do themselves gave them strength to endure the challenges of Church membership in their home country and to go forth bearing "exceedingly great and glorious tidings, in truth,"[18] as they continue building the Lord's kingdom in Laos.

During the time we have not been able to attend the temple, have we each relied upon the covenants we made in the temple to set a clear, unchanging course of direction in our lives? These covenants, if kept, give us vision and expectations regarding the future and a clear determination to qualify to receive all that the Lord has promised through our faithfulness.

I invite you to seek the power God wants to give you. I testify that as we seek for this power, we will be blessed with a greater understanding of the love our Heavenly Father has for us.

I testify that because Heavenly Father loves you and me, He sent His Beloved Son, Jesus Christ, to be our Savior and Redeemer. I testify of Jesus Christ, He who has all power,[19] and do so in the name of Jesus Christ, amen.

Notes

1. See Russell M. Nelson, "Protect the Spiritual Power Line," *Ensign*, Nov. 1984, 30–32.
2. See Russell M. Nelson, "Ministering with the Power and Authority of God," *Ensign* or *Liahona*, May 2018, 68–75.
3. See Russell M. Nelson, "Closing Remarks," *Ensign* or *Liahona*, May 2019, 112.
4. See Russell M. Nelson, "Ministering with the Power and Authority of God," 68–69.

5. See Russell M. Nelson, "Go Forward in Faith," *Ensign* or *Liahona*, May 2020, 115.
6. Russell M. Nelson, "Go Forward in Faith," 115.
7. See Doctrine and Covenants 9:7–9.
8. Richard G. Scott, "For Peace at Home," *Ensign* or *Liahona*, May 2013, 30.
9. "Microwaves use microwave sound energy waves to heat up food or liquids. There has to be something inside the microwave to absorb these waves. Otherwise, the microwave will absorb the waves instead. The waves will heat up the microwave's cooking chamber, trying to find something to be absorbed by. The waves will eventually reach the microwave's magnetron, which is the source for the microwaves. The magnetron cannot handle a huge amount of power, so it continues to send it to other parts of the microwave. Running a microwave with nothing in it will damage the magnetron and other parts of the microwave as well. In a worst case scenario, the microwave parts will overheat and possibly catch fire" (Abacus Appliance Service Corporation, "Will I Destroy My Microwave If It Runs Empty?" Aug. 16, 2012, abacusappliance.com; see also Julie R. Thomson, "13 Things You Should Never Put in the Microwave," June 13, 2014, huffpost.com).
10. See 1 Nephi 15:24.
11. 2 Timothy 1:7.
12. Luke 2:40.
13. Luke 2:52.
14. Luke 4:32.
15. See Matthew 4:1–11; Luke 4:1–14; Doctrine and Covenants 20:22.
16. See Doctrine and Covenants 109:22.
17. Doctrine and Covenants 109:22.
18. Doctrine and Covenants 109:23.
19. See Matthew 28:18.

WAITING ON THE LORD

ELDER JEFFREY R. HOLLAND
Of the Quorum of the Twelve Apostles

My beloved brothers and sisters, we are all eager—no one more than I—to hear concluding remarks from our beloved prophet, President Russell M. Nelson. This has been a marvelous conference, but it is the second time that COVID-19 has altered our traditional proceedings. We are so tired of this contagion, we feel like tearing our hair out. And apparently, some of my Brethren have already taken that course of action. Please know that we do pray constantly for those who have been affected in any way, especially for any who have lost loved ones. Everyone agrees that this has gone on much, much too long.

How long do we wait for relief from hardships that come upon us? What about enduring personal trials while we wait and wait, and help seems so slow in coming? Why the delay when burdens seem more than we can bear?

While asking such questions, we can, if we try, hear another's cry echoing from a dank, dark prison cell during one of the coldest winters then on record in that locale.

"O God, where art thou?" we hear from the depths of Liberty Jail. "And where is the pavilion that covereth thy hiding place? How long shall thy hand be stayed?"[1] How long, O Lord, how long?

So, we are not the first nor will we be the last to ask such questions when sorrows bear down on us or an ache in our heart goes on and on. I am not now speaking of pandemics or prisons but of you, your family, and your neighbors who face any number of such challenges. I speak of the yearning of many who would like to be married and aren't or who are married and wish the relationship were a little more celestial. I speak of those who have to deal with the unwanted appearance of a serious medical condition—perhaps an incurable one—or who face a lifelong battle with a genetic defect that has no remedy. I speak of the continuing struggle with emotional and mental health challenges that weigh heavily on the souls of so many who suffer with them, and on the hearts of those who love and suffer with them. I speak of the poor, whom the Savior told us never to forget, and I speak of you waiting for the return of a child, no matter what the age, who has chosen a path different from the one you prayed he or she would take.

Furthermore, I acknowledge that even this long list of things for which we might wait personally does not attempt to address the large economic, political, and social concerns that confront us collectively. Our Father in Heaven clearly expects us to address these wrenching public issues as well as the personal ones, but there will be times in our lives when even our best spiritual effort and earnest, pleading prayers do not yield the victories for which we have yearned, whether that be regarding the large global matters or the small personal ones. So while we work and wait together for the answers to some of our prayers, I offer you my apostolic promise that they are heard and they are answered, though perhaps not at the time or in the way we wanted. But they are *always* answered at the time and in the way an omniscient and eternally compassionate parent should answer them. My beloved brothers and sisters, please understand that He who never sleeps nor slumbers[2] cares for the happiness and ultimate exaltation of His children above all else that a divine being has to do. He is pure love, gloriously personified, and Merciful Father is His name.

"Well, if this is the case," you might say, "shouldn't His love and mercy simply part our personal Red Seas and allow us to walk through our troubles on dry ground? Shouldn't He send 21st-century seagulls winging in from somewhere to gobble up all of our pesky 21st-century crickets?"

The answer to such questions is "Yes, God can provide miracles instantaneously, but sooner or later we learn that the times and seasons of our mortal journey are His and His alone to direct." He administers that calendar to every one of us individually. For every infirm man healed instantly as he waits to enter the Pool of Bethesda,[3] someone else will spend 40 years in the desert waiting to enter the promised land.[4] For every Nephi and Lehi divinely protected by an encircling flame of fire for their faith,[5] we have an

Abinadi burned at a stake of flaming fire for his.[6] And we remember that the same Elijah who in an instant called down fire from heaven to bear witness against the priests of Baal[7] is the same Elijah who endured a period when there was no rain for years and who, for a time, was fed only by the skimpy sustenance that could be carried in a raven's claw.[8] By my estimation, that can't have been anything we would call a "happy meal."

The point? The point is that faith means trusting God in good times and bad, even if that includes some suffering until we see His arm revealed in our behalf.[9] That can be difficult in our modern world when many have come to believe that the highest good in life is to avoid all suffering, that no one should ever anguish over anything.[10] But that belief will never lead us to "the measure of the stature of the fulness of Christ."[11]

With apologies to Elder Neal A. Maxwell for daring to modify and enlarge something he once said, I too suggest that "one's life . . . cannot be both faith-filled and stress-free." It simply will not work "to glide naively through life," saying as we sip another glass of lemonade, "Lord, give me all thy choicest virtues, but be certain not to give me grief, nor sorrow, nor pain, nor opposition. Please do not let anyone dislike me or betray me, and above all, do not ever let me feel forsaken by Thee or those I love. In fact, Lord, be careful to keep me from all the experiences that made Thee divine. And then, when the rough sledding by everyone else is over, please let me come and dwell with Thee, where I can boast about how similar our strengths and our characters are as I float along on my cloud of comfortable Christianity."[12]

My beloved brothers and sisters, Christianity is comforting, but it is often not comfortable. The path to holiness and happiness here and hereafter is a long and sometimes rocky one. It takes time and tenacity to walk it. But, of course, the reward for doing so is monumental. This truth is taught clearly and persuasively in the 32nd chapter of Alma in the Book of Mormon. There this great high priest teaches that if the word of God is planted in our hearts as a mere seed, and if we care enough to water, weed, nourish, and encourage it, it will *in the future* bear fruit "which is most precious, . . . sweet above all that is sweet," the consuming of which leads to a condition of no more thirst and no more hunger.[13]

Many lessons are taught in this remarkable chapter, but central to them all is the axiom that the seed has to be nourished and we must wait for it to mature; we "*[look] forward* with an eye of faith to the fruit thereof."[14] Our harvest, Alma says, comes "by and by."[15] Little wonder that he concludes his remarkable instruction by repeating three times a call for *diligence* and *patience* in nurturing the word of God in our hearts, "*waiting,*" as he says, with "long-suffering . . . for the tree to bring forth fruit unto you."[16]

COVID and cancer, doubt and dismay, financial trouble and family trials. When will these burdens be lifted? The answer is "by and by."[17] And whether that be a short period or a long one is not always ours to say, but by the grace of God, the blessings will come to those who hold fast to the gospel of Jesus Christ. That issue was settled in a very private garden and on a very public hill in Jerusalem long ago.

As we now hear our beloved prophet close this conference, may we remember, as Russell Nelson has demonstrated all of his life, that those who "*wait upon the Lord* shall renew their strength [and] shall mount up with wings as eagles; they shall run, and not be weary; . . . they shall walk, and not faint."[18] I pray that "by and by"—soon or late—those blessings will come to every one of you who seeks relief from your sorrow and freedom from your grief. I bear witness of God's love and of the Restoration of His glorious gospel, which is, in one way or another, the answer to every issue we face in life. In the redeeming name of the Lord Jesus Christ, amen.

Notes

1. Doctrine and Covenants 121:1–2.
2. See Psalm 121:4.
3. See John 5:2–9.
4. See Numbers 32:13; Deuteronomy 2:7; Joshua 5:6.
5. See Helaman 5:20–52.
6. See Mosiah 17.
7. See 1 Kings 18:17–40.
8. See 1 Kings 17:1–7.
9. See Doctrine and Covenants 123:17.

10. See Rankin Wilbourne and Brian Gregor, "Jesus Didn't Suffer to Prove a Philosophical Point," *Christianity Today*, Sept. 20, 2019, christianitytoday.com.
11. Ephesians 4:13.
12. Elder Jeffrey R. Holland's modification of Elder Neal A. Maxwell's text; see Neal A. Maxwell, "Lest Ye Be Wearied and Faint in Your Minds," *Ensign*, May 1991, 88.
13. Alma 32:42.
14. Alma 32:40; emphasis added.
15. Alma 32:42.
16. Alma 32:43; emphasis added; see also Alma 32:41–42.
17. Alma 32:42.
18. Isaiah 40:31; emphasis added; see also Isaiah 40:28–30.

A NEW NORMAL

PRESIDENT RUSSELL M. NELSON

President of The Church of Jesus Christ of Latter-day Saints

My dear brothers and sisters, these two days of general conference have been glorious! I agree with Elder Jeffrey R. Holland. As he mentioned, the messages, the prayers, and the music have all been inspired by the Lord. I am grateful to all who have participated in any way.

Throughout the proceedings, I have pictured you in my mind listening to conference. I have asked the Lord to help me understand what you are feeling, worrying about, or trying to resolve. I have wondered what I might say to conclude this conference that would send you forth with the optimism about the future that I know the Lord wants you to feel.

We live in a glorious age, foreseen by prophets for centuries. This is the dispensation when no spiritual blessing will be withheld from the righteous.[1] Despite the world's commotion,[2] the Lord would have us look forward to the future "with joyful anticipation."[3] Let us not spin our wheels in the memories of yesterday. The gathering of Israel moves forward. The Lord Jesus Christ directs the affairs of His Church, and it *will* achieve its divine objectives.

The challenge for you and me is to make certain that each of *us* will achieve his or her divine potential. Today we often hear about "a new normal." If you really want to embrace a new normal, I invite you to turn your heart, mind, and soul increasingly to our Heavenly Father and His Son, Jesus Christ. Let that be *your* new normal.

Embrace your new normal by repenting daily. Seek to be increasingly pure in thought, word, and deed. Minister to others. Keep an eternal perspective. Magnify your callings. And whatever your challenges, my dear brothers and sisters, live each day so that *you* are more prepared to meet your Maker.[4]

That is why we have temples. The Lord's ordinances and covenants prepare us for eternal life, the greatest of all of God's blessings.[5] As you know, the COVID pandemic required a temporary closure of our temples. Then we commenced a carefully coordinated, phased reopening. With phase 2 now in place in many temples, thousands of couples have been sealed and thousands have received their own endowments just in the past few months. We look forward to the day when all worthy members of the Church can again serve their ancestors and worship in a holy temple.

Now I am pleased to announce plans for the construction of six new temples to be built in the following locations: Tarawa, Kiribati; Port Vila, Vanuatu; Lindon, Utah; Greater Guatemala City, Guatemala; São Paulo East, Brazil; and Santa Cruz, Bolivia.

As we build and maintain these temples, we pray that each of you will build and maintain yourself so you can be worthy to enter the holy temple.

Now, my dear brothers and sisters, I bless you to be filled with the peace of the Lord Jesus Christ. His peace is beyond all mortal understanding.[6] I bless you with an increased desire and ability to obey the laws of God. I promise that as you do, you will be showered with blessings, including greater courage, increased personal revelation, sweeter harmony in your homes, and joy even amid uncertainty.

May we go forward together to fulfill our divine mandate—that of preparing ourselves and the world for the Second Coming of the Lord. I so pray, with my expression of love for you, in the sacred name of Jesus Christ, amen.

Notes

1. See Doctrine and Covenants 121:26–29.
2. See Doctrine and Covenants 45:26; 88:91.
3. *Teachings of Presidents of the Church: Joseph Smith* (2007), 513.
4. See Alma 12:24; 34:32.
5. See Doctrine and Covenants 14:7.
6. See Philippians 4:7.